Better Homes and Gardens®

decks
Step-by-Step

Meredith® Books
Des Moines, Iowa

TABLE OF CONTENTS

Planning
YOUR DECK PROJECT — 6

Building
A BASIC DECK — 24

Customizing
YOUR DECK — 66

Deck
VARIATIONS 88

Tools,
MATERIALS, AND TECHNIQUES 112

Finishes,
MAINTENANCE, AND REPAIRS 140

INTRODUCTION

Decks are a do-it-yourselfer's dream. If you're an amateur builder, even if you're completely new to carpentry, you can design and build a deck that will give you years of enjoyment. You need only a modest set of tools, a few basic skills, and the patience to work one step at a time.

There are many reasons for building a deck. Some of the more common ones are to get additional outdoor living space for you and your family, and to create a versatile area (an outdoor room, really) for casual or formal entertaining, quiet relaxation, communing with nature, and children's play. A deck will make your yard more attractive, and if you plan its appearance carefully, it will become a natural extension of the architecture of your home and an inviting transition to the surrounding landscape. Besides, a deck can add substantially to the value of your property. According to the National Home Builders Association, you can get up to 75 percent of its cost back when you sell your home.

A deck is not only fun to use, it can be fun to build. Most decks can be built in several weekends, and you don't need to worry about finishing everything all at once. You may have self-imposed deadlines (such as the date for your first deck party), but unlike an interior remodeling project, such as a kitchen makeover, you can leave most aspects of deck construction undone without disrupting daily life in your home.

Careful planning is your key to success. A deck, at its most basic level, is simply a horizontal surface attached to the exterior of your home. But it should be much more than that. In fact, if you don't take it further, you probably won't use it much. Get some ideas from the whole family so the features that everyone wants will be part of your plan and you can build a deck that everyone will enjoy.

HOW TO USE THIS BOOK

As you become more familiar with the way decks are built, you'll find the project more rewarding. That's where this book comes in: It provides the information you need to become proficient in each stage of building your deck.

You'll find definitions of terms associated with the structure of a deck on page 8. Although you don't have to know what a header is in order to attach one, a knowledge of deck construction and terminology will help. You'll be able to communicate more clearly when you order materials, seek advice from home-center staff, or discuss plans with building inspectors.

This chapter also helps you answer other questions: Where should it go? How big should it be? What should it look like? Along the way, you'll find photos of features you may want to incorporate into your own design.

The next chapter, "Building a Basic Deck," provides complete step-by-step instructions for constructing a safe, sturdy deck. You'll learn how to attach a ledger to your house, lay out the site, set footings and posts, and frame and finish the deck.

If you want to make your deck more useful as well as increase its comfort, you'll find some ideas in "Customizing Your Deck." You'll see how different decking patterns can create a striking look for a deck. That chapter also describes hidden fasteners that can give decking a clean, more modern look. You'll find railings, planters, seating, and overhead structures that can add to the look and function of your deck. The chapter also describes how to make the features part of your deck.

The chapter on "Deck Variations" includes ideas for tailoring the shape of your deck (or other aspects of its design) to particular sites. Some of the variations include modular decks, wraparounds, multilevel designs, decks for entryways, and ideas for second-story decks and other elevated structures.

And any time you need to brush up on a particular skill or material needed for your deck, you can turn to the next chapter, "Tools, Materials, and Techniques."

The last chapter, "Finishes, Maintenance, and Repairs," shows how to protect the finished results of all your work and to properly maintain your deck.

TIP BOXES

There's a box headed "You'll Need" with each project that provides an estimate of how long a project will take and what skills and tools you'll need. Other boxes have tips on cutting costs, organizing the job, and tricks of the trade from experts. Pay special attention to "Caution" boxes. They warn you when a step requires special care and can help you avoid injuring yourself or damaging the job at hand.

Local communities enact building codes to establish standards for safety, aesthetics, and durability. "Working to code" means knowing and understanding those local building codes, and complying with them as you build your project.

Many building codes consider a deck to be a permanent addition, so there are regulations that define footing depths, material choices, and fence heights. Check with your local building department before you start your project.

Even as a private individual working on a deck for your own use on your own property, you have the same responsibilities to satisfy building authorities as a professional carpenter or contractor. You should submit plans to your building department for approval and obtain a building permit. Depending on its policies, the building department may also want to inspect your work periodically to make sure you're following the plans they approved. Failing to comply with codes could result in an order to remove what you've built.

Not everyone is required to get a building permit. But it's up to you, not the authorities, to find out what laws cover your project.

Besides building codes, you may find the following ordinances that can affect your deck design.

Zoning ordinances
These regulate the use of property and the placement of structures on it. They can establish minimum setbacks from property lines, easements, and the size of your deck. In recent years, many communities have established limits on the amount of deck surface because large areas of hardscape increase the flow of runoff into storm sewers.

Deed restrictions
Some communities adopt deed restrictions to control property values or architectural style. These may

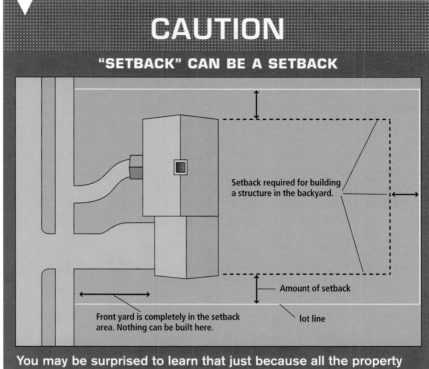

CAUTION
"SETBACK" CAN BE A SETBACK

Setback required for building a structure in the backyard.

Amount of setback

lot line

Front yard is completely in the setback area. Nothing can be built here.

You may be surprised to learn that just because all the property inside your property lines belongs to you, that doesn't mean you can put your deck right up next to them. Local building codes or zoning ordinances may require you to observe "setback" requirements—a specified distance from adjoining property lines. Check with your local officials before drawing any plans.

restrict the style of your deck and the materials you can use.

Easements and rights of way
These rules guarantee access by utilities to their lines and may restrict your ability to build a deck where you want to. Before you get too far into your planning, have your utilities come flag the path of underground lines through your property. Most will do this for free and with one call to a central agency.

The procedures in this book will satisfy most local codes, but codes can vary widely—and they can change from time to time. Always check with your city or county building department.

Working with inspectors
To avoid unnecessary questions about your plans, get as much information as possible about local requirements and incorporate what you learn into your plan before you take it in for approval. Your building department may have publications that list requirements for the type of project you have planned.

Go to your building department with a plan to be approved; don't expect the inspectors to plan the job for you. Present your plan with neatly drawn diagrams and a complete list of the materials you will use.

Be sure you understand clearly at what stages of your project you need to have inspections. Do not cover up plumbing or electrical installations that need to be inspected.

Take time to do high-quality work. Inspectors often are wary of homeowners because so many do shoddy work. Show the inspector you are serious by following your approved plan and completing the work correctly.

Planning
YOUR DECK PROJECT

A deck should be an expression of the way you live, whether it's for winding up or winding down. It can be a quiet place for morning coffee or the last few chapters in your favorite book, an outdoor family room for catching up on conversation, a dining spot for two (or twenty), or the hot spot for weekend neighborhood nightlife.

A properly planned deck will be tough enough to stand up to the rigors of children's play and assaults by the outdoor elements and versatile enough for gatherings of almost any size. You can have all that enjoyable outdoor space, and you can create it yourself.

Planning and designing a deck starts with the same question as planning spaces inside your home: What will you do in your outdoor room? If your needs are simple and the backyard small, you can get by with a modest deck– one that's 10×12 feet may do. Lavish entertainment demands more room, and perhaps an outdoor kitchen. Stairs leading to other levels will handle a crowd. "Form follows function" may seem a slightly worn-out phrase, but it's still useful in deck design. Think about function first. The fun will follow.

COMPLEMENT AND CONTRAST

Integrating all the elements into a harmonious deck will create a place where you'll want to spend time. This deck has both a large platform for festive parties and a smaller space for family dining. The outdoor kitchen doesn't interfere with natural traffic patterns, but is still convenient to both areas. Its color and texture add style. Stuccoed block and light, airy furnishings create an eye-catching accent against the rich backdrop of redwood and foliage.

PUT IN SOME PERSONALITY

Railings are a great, inexpensive way to customize your deck. This railing, woven from maple rails and branches, complies with local building codes. Check with your building inspector before installing any railing.

BUILD FOR BEAUTY

A small deck doesn't have to look like a pallet's first cousin stuck on the back of a house. That's the kind of deck that often sits unused. Containers with plants add color and texture and ease the transition from the deck to the rest of the landscape. Flowers and foliage make any deck a stand-out. Outdoor curtains hung on a beam track provide moveable shade—a clever solution for a space too small for an umbrella table.

THE TERMINOLOGY OF DECKS

A deck is essentially an outdoor floor supported by a frame, posts, and footings secured in the ground, made in layers and built from the ground up. The following terms define all of the important components of a typical deck. Specific types of decks may differ; such variations will be discussed later in the book.

Beams or girders: Hefty framing members (usually 4×, 6×, or doubled 2× stock) attached horizontally to the posts to support the joists.

Decking: 2× or 5/4 stock attached to the joists to form the floor of the deck.

Footings: Concrete columns below grade that support the posts and, thus, the deck. On sites where the soil freezes and thaws, concrete is poured in a form inserted in a hole that's dug to frost depth. Ask your building department for footing depths in your area.

Joists: Horizontal framing members (usually 2× stock) fastened on top of the beam or flush with the ledger to support the decking. A header is fastened to the ends of the deck's interior joists. Rim joists or end joists are the outermost joists perpendicular to the ledger.

Ledger: A header attached to the house to support one side of the deck.

Piers: (not illustrated) Precast concrete pyramids made to be set on in-ground footings, or where frost heave is not a factor, directly on the ground to support posts.

Post anchors: Metal framing connectors which attach posts to piers or footings. They raise the base of the posts slightly above the top of the footing, protecting them from water and insect damage.

Posts: Timbers (usually 4× or 6×) set vertically to support the deck framing. Posts are used on all but the shortest decks. The posts can be cut off below the deck surface, or they may rise above the surface to provide

support for the railing. Posts may rest on top of concrete footings or they can be set in the hole before the concrete is poured.

Rails: Horizontal components of railings that provide a safety barrier and handhold for stairs or along the sides of the deck.

Railing: The assembly made of rails, rail posts, cap rails, and balusters or spindles. The balusters, the smallest vertical components, are positioned to fill the space between the top and bottom rails and between rail posts. Maximum baluster spacing for child safety is 4 inches.

Risers: Boards that enclose the vertical spaces between stairway treads. Risers are often omitted on deck steps and other exterior steps.

Stringers: Long diagonal framing members (usually 2×12s) that support stairs. The stair treads are attached to the stringers.

Treads: The horizontal, stepping surfaces of a stairway.

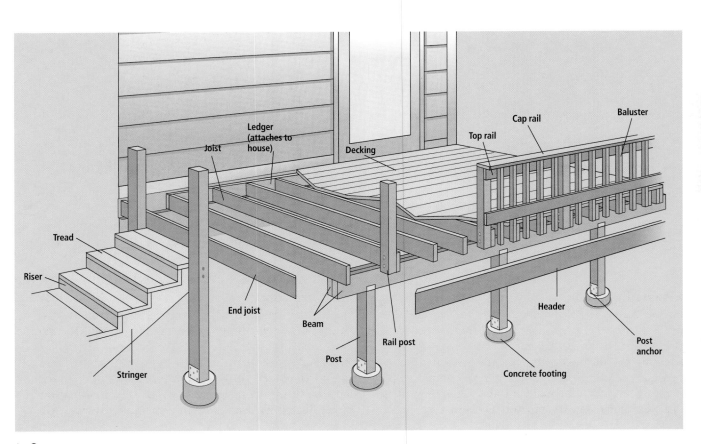

DECK CONFIGURATIONS

Decks can be almost any shape imaginable, but the shape of your deck should not be an arbitrary choice. Design the shape of your deck to conform to the terrain of your landscape, the architecture of your home, and how you plan to use the deck.

The least complicated installation will feature a ground-level deck—ideal for a flat yard and single-story home. Because this design hugs the ground, codes may not require a railing. Combine overlapping sections to make a deck cascade down a gentle slope.

Beyond the simple ground-level platform, decks fall into the three categories illustrated on this page.

Wraparound deck

This design faces two or more sides of the house. It's ideal when you want areas for quiet activities (a getaway outside the bedroom, for example) and large parties (adjacent to the kitchen) all in one deck. Wraparound decks also offer a solution for backyards that get different amounts of sunlight at different times of the day.

Wraparound decks offer great versatility for families who want their outdoor space for a variety of needs. You can build a wraparound deck as a single ground-level platform, as a multilevel structure, or as a raised deck that provides second-story access.

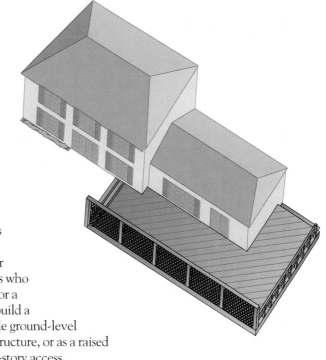

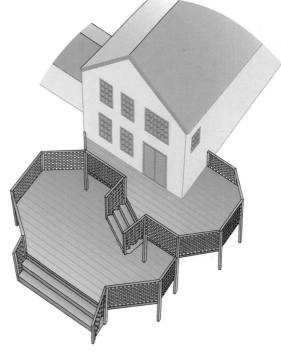

Elevated deck

An elevated deck can provide access to upper-level rooms or create a level recreational or entertainment space on sloping terrain. The least complicated version of this structure is a single platform supported by posts with lengths that follow the contours of the ground to keep the platform level. You can build one also to take advantage of a spectacular view you might not otherwise see.

Multilevel deck

This design, which can have sections with different sizes and shapes, provides a practical solution to sloping terrain. You don't have to build a multilevel deck on a slope. You can build one section of this structure on flat ground and use it to provide a convenient transition to a deck on an upper level of your home. Consider this design when you need different deck areas for different outdoor activities.

Before starting you might assume that siting the deck is easy; that impression might change after some on-site research. Your first site choice may meet some requirements but not others.

A deck should not exist in isolation. It should relate to the architectural style of your home as well as to other aspects of your site that aren't necessarily visible. The ideal location for your deck will provide easy access from indoors and out, make the best use of natural views, and give you enough privacy that you don't feel you're on display. The proper site should also take advantage of sun and shade patterns, prevailing breezes, and other natural conditions to provide maximum comfort and usability.

Take a look at these conditions before you commit to your initial plans. Inventory your site and list its assets and liabilities. Then use your notes to draw a site analysis. You may have to evaluate a number of options, but if you make those decisions now, you'll probably avoid building a deck that you won't use much.

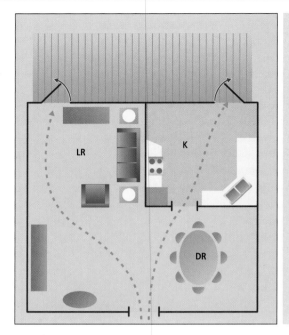

LANDSCAPING YOUR DECK

Even a perfectly planned deck can look like an intrusion onto your landscape. Make your deck seem like a natural extension of the yard with a thoughtful landscaping plan. A perennial border garden, for example, will ease the transition from the deck to the yard. Shrubs can camouflage the deck framing and that gaping empty space beneath it. Baskets, pots, and planters will unify the entire scene with color and texture.

A well-designed deck should be visible from inside the house, easy to get to, and similar in its purpose to the uses of the adjacent interior room. Interior designers call these factors *access* and *compatibility*; they can determine whether you use your deck or whether it sits idle.

Visual and physical access

You have to see your deck for it to invite you outside. But if your proposed site doesn't beckon you outside, don't move the deck just yet. Include new widows or doors in your plans. You don't need to see the whole deck from inside the house. Just a glimpse is often more effective than a view of the complete deck.

Make the view attractive with accents you can see from the inside— geometric decking patterns, a decorative railing insert, or container gardens are attractive visual enticements. And if you can see these attractions from more than one room, so much the better. If you can't, just design your deck space so the largest view is from the room that adjoins it.

Looking out at your deck isn't the only thing that matters, of course. You have to be able to get to it easily. To make sure the pathway to the deck

is open and free of obstructions, make a sketch of the routes people use when walking through your home (above). If the location you choose creates traffic jams, make alterations. For example, although a deck next to your kitchen might seem ideal for outdoor dining, it may make the traffic in your cooking space unbearable. Moving a door to a side wall can redirect the traffic away from the work areas.

Compatibility

The success of your deck may depend on what goes on in its nearest indoor room because you will tend to use your deck more if its use is similar to that of the interior room next to it. For example, a small deck for coffee or morning conversation would feel just right outside your bedroom. But that would be the wrong place for a large party deck.

For outdoor dining, put the deck close to the kitchen. Plan party areas close to the family room or other public rooms of the house. For private space, limit access—and shield your space behind hedges or fencing.

Inventory your site

Before you finalize your plans, inventory your property to see how the terrain and climate might affect the location of your deck.

Terrain is the characteristic which will probably most affect your deck site. Deck construction is relatively simple on flat land. A slope might require grading, a retaining wall, or an elevated deck. Also, a deck can make a hillside an opportunity instead of an obstacle. High slopes can offer magnificent views. Land that slopes up from a deck site can provide natural privacy and shelter from the wind.

Terrain can affect temperature, too. A deck on a hill will feel warmer than one at the end of an incline because cooler air flows downhill. And if you trap that cool air with a retaining wall or a fence, your deck might feel cold after sunset.

You'll want your deck shaded when you use it, so track shade patterns by driving stakes in the yard. If your proposed site is naturally shaded, your decisions will be easier to make. But if you need additional shade, you can make some. Trees and other plants can shade a site that gets too much afternoon sun. So can an umbrella table or pergola, especially if you construct a slatted roof to filter out the sunlight. Vines climbing up a lattice wall can cool off a site that gets hot in the late afternoon.

Note prevailing winds, too—you'll want your deck sheltered from strong winds so you may have to build or plant a windbreak. Be wary of solid fences —they create low-pressure pockets that pull the wind into the very area you want protected. Louvers and lattice are good options—closed enough to add privacy, but open enough to let filtered wind through. You can't chart the rain, of course, but you can protect yourself with solid roofing over a part of your deck. Or add an awning which you can retract when the skies are clear.

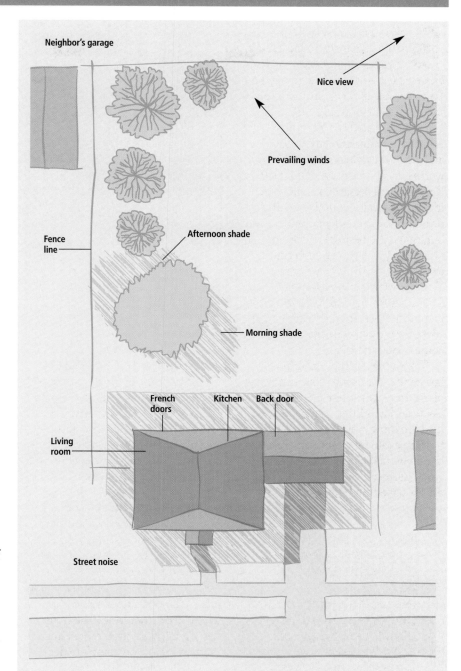

DRAW A SITE ANALYSIS.

Put all your notes about your landscape on a site analysis. Start with a sketch of your yard and house, including the doors and windows, as well as utility hookups, walkways, bushes and trees. Then show views you want to keep and those you want to block out. Note the movement of the sun and where shade falls during different parts of the day. Add every detail that could affect the deck location—prevailing winds, septic tanks and utility lines, setbacks, and downspouts. When puting your deck plans on paper, lay tracing paper over the site analysis to sketch possible shapes and locations for the deck.

Like many other questions about building a deck, the answer to how large it should be will pretty much fall into place once you've decided how you're going to use the deck. The chart below shows rough estimates of the space required for different activities. Use these as a guide to sizing your deck.

If your deck will have several uses (a play area for the kids, space for dining, an area for sunning) you may be tempted to make it as big as possible. But multiple functions don't always call for more deck. Sometimes a small design element, such as a level change, can better isolate functional zones. However, if you plan to have a one-level deck, use the high end of your size estimate. Adding more space now is less expensive than adding it later, and the last thing you want is a cramped deck. If your budget is tight, plan a deck that you can build in stages, adding elements as you can afford them, but keeping the overall design intact.

A BREEZY BOARDWALK

If you're designing a single level deck large enough for both small and large gatherings—but you want to dress up the platform inexpensively—add a perimeter boardwalk. This narrow extension gives you a little more room at a fraction of the cost of an additional platform. And it gives guests a way to move to the far end of the deck without passing through the main activity sections. Define spaces casually with moveable furnishings. The hammock chairs hung from the pergola on this deck are a clever addition to informal seating.

HOW BIG?

Activity	Space required
Dining for four for six to eight	About 10×10 ft. 12×12 ft.
Conversation area for six	About 10×10 ft.
Single reclining chair	About 4×7 ft.
Two recliners	About 7×7 ft.
Basic cooking area with grill	A space about 6 ft. square, more for counter, island or large serving table
Rectangular table	An area 5 to 6 ft. wider and longer than the table itself
A round table for six	Circular area, 9 ft. in diameter
Pathways, real and imaginary	3½ to 4 ft. wide at all points

CUT DOWN ON MOWING

A wraparound redwood deck with a wrought-iron railing transforms a narrow, unused side yard from lawn space into an open-air veranda. It's small but still has plenty of room for casual conversation. Such a deck can expand your living area with style and will reduce your lawn mowing time.

MULTIPLE MANDATES

French doors from the family room open onto this deck with multiple levels sized for different uses. Next to the house, the first tier offers a quiet vantage point for taking in the open landscape, protected by the rear wall. The second and third platforms provide extra room for larger gatherings.

SECOND-STORY RESPITE

This elevated platform was designed for casual moments outside the master bedroom. It's only about 6 feet wide, but just large enough to provide a spectacular way to start (or end) each day.

TEST THE SITE SIZE

Sizing things up (or down). To test the size of your deck site, rope off the area (or outline it with a hose). Then bring in the furniture, including the barbecue grill, lounge chairs, tables, and recliners.

Adjust the size until you're sure the deck will have room for all of your planned activities. Then step back and consider its scale.

A deck should be proportionate to the house and grounds. If your deck is small, you probably won't have much of a scale problem. It's a large deck that often looks too big next to a modest home. Start with a design that fits the uses you envision, then scale back to fit the limits of your budget and terrain.

DESIGNING FOR DINING

You don't have to spend a fortune to enjoy the taste of outdoor cooking and dining. Even a basic charcoal grill and a small serving area at the edge of the deck will get you started. More elaborate (and more costly) designs can include rotisseries and refrigerators, as well as storage for utensils and a handy prep sink.

Privacy will help make you feel more comfortable and at home on your deck because you won't feel exposed.

Stand in each section of the trial deck site you've outlined on the ground (previous page). Sit in all the chairs you've moved in for the test. Can your neighbors see your every move? Is your deck open to views from the sidewalk or street? Even if the neighbors' homes aren't close, do you feel unprotected and exposed? If so, you need more privacy.

Building the deck on an unexposed side of the house may solve the problem. But if your yard doesn't offer an architectural fix, add screening—a privacy fence, a wall, or trees and shrubs. You can apply different solutions to different parts of the deck.

Spaces planned for activities, such as reading, conversation, sunbathing, or meditation should be well screened, as should pools and spas. Build walls or high fences, or plant dense rows of evergreen shrubs.

Areas for large gatherings or children's play don't need as much privacy. Use partial screens—trees, latticework, board-on-board fences, or low seat walls. Train vines onto a screen—the leaves will ultimately hide the screen and make it seem like nature put it there.

DON'T FENCE YOURSELF IN

Place screens strategically.
Before you encircle your deck with shrubs or a solid fence, locate the spots where other people can see you. Then block the most revealing views first. Try to enhance your privacy without barricading yourself in. The closer to the deck, the more privacy. The further away, the less. Strategy helps, and so will lattice, pickets, and ornamental iron fencing. These seem friendly because they don't block the view completely.

BUILD THE SCENE
Solid fences make perfect neutral backdrops for artful accents, floral arrangements, green plants, and vines. Tack chicken wire or partially driven screws into a solid fence to give your vines a footing.

PROPERTY-LINE PRIVACY
Adding privacy along a property line can be tricky; your neighbors might not like the look of their side of your solid fence. Let lattice come to your rescue. It looks a lot more friendly, especially when hung with a flowering vine.

PRIVACY WITH STYLE
Fencing is functional, but planning it from the beginning helps integrate it aesthetically into the overall style of your deck. A curved surface always softens the effect of a structure.

DESIGNING STRUCTURES OVERHEAD

Overhead structures, such as pergolas and arbors, are usually made for shade, but that's not their only use. They also can enhance the aesthetics of the deck and complete the sense of enclosure.

Just as interior ceilings help make us feel at home indoors, outdoor areas need some kind of physical limit overhead—but just the right amount—to feel comfortable. For example, space for large groups can have a high overhead structure (or none at all). Private spaces, used for dining, conversing, or relaxing, feel more inviting with a lower ceiling.

An arbor, pergola, canopy, or even a retractable awning can also protect you from the elements, especially harsh sunlight. Slats in an overhead roof can shade the deck when and where you want it. With careful attention to the spacing, orientation, and angle of the slats, you can control the amount of shade it provides.

No matter what kind of overhead you build, integrate it into your overall design. Pick up some detail of your home—a molding or post style, the pitch of the roof, an accent color, or building material. Linking the structure to your home can turn an average-looking deck into a unique addition to your landscape.

A LAYER OF LATH
Overheads are commonly roofed with dimensioned lumber. Other materials, such as bamboo or willow branches, will shade your deck, enclose it, and set it apart from the rest.

NATURE'S ROOM
Most overheads will look better, and function more effectively if they enclose a selected area of the deck. Choose the space you want to cover and experiment with the slat or rafter spacing.

INTEGRATED DESIGN
Look to the style of your home for design clues. Color is useful, but so are the lines of your house. Repeating such elements will make your deck seem planned right from the start.

WHAT'S UP?

Designing overhead comfort
Stand out in your proposed deck site and look up. If you see open sky, you may need an overhead structure—even if you don't need shade. Tree branches 15 to 20 feet off the ground might make an intimate table for two feel exposed.

Set up a table with an umbrella to make the site feel more cozy.

Small, private areas usually need a cover 10 to 12 feet above the deck surface. Party space will feel right with a 15 to 20-foot ceiling. Shelter at least one-third of the surface area of your deck.

DESIGNING FOR STYLE

Questions about style intimidate many homeowners. Most of us don't consider ourselves landscape designers. But look at it this way: You've designed the interior rooms of your house, so there's no reason you can't design your outdoor room too.

Follow a theme when planning the style of your deck. You can organize your deck along what's considered formal or informal lines or you can establish an oriental, southwestern, or mediterranean theme. Easier yet, bring in the colors, textures, and culture of your area. Be cool, serene, and comfortable with a contemporary scheme that uses bold shapes and colors, sleek lines, and geometric arrangements. Or forget about categories altogether and develop a style that incorporates eclectic elements that otherwise would seem incongruous. You may find they fit perfectly on your deck.

Style is in the details, especially the decking, railings, and stairs. If the style of your deck reflects your personality, you'll use it more often and enjoy it more.

ACCENT THE RAILING
Railings are the most visible element of your deck; they make an instant design statement. Add appeal by inserting accents in your railing design. A corniced panel, geometric accent, or even prefab rail caps and finials can add pizzazz to an otherwise mundane lineup of 2×2 balusters.

PLANT THE EDGES
No matter what style you choose, put plantings at the edges of your deck. Carefully chosen containers can cover the edges of the structure and create a transition into the surrounding landscape.

DISCOVERING YOUR STYLE

If you can't decide how you want your deck to look, the best place to start looking for ideas is right around your home. Your neighborhood can often provide you with just the clues you need. Tour one or two neighboring blocks and make notes of what you like. You'll be surprised at what you haven't noticed before. Clip photos from landscape magazines, and look through books about outdoor design. Then spread your notes and photo clips out on the dining-room table and incorporate whatever appeals to you into your own design.

HARMONIZE YOUR LANDSCAPE

Individual elements in a good design create a unified whole. Base design continuity on the lines and colors of your house. For example, a platform deck running parallel to a ranch home creates a harmony of horizontal lines. A deck full of angles will fit nicely with a west-coast modular, but not on the back of a three-story Victorian house. Duplicate stained cedar shingles in your railing design and look for color cues, too. Paint, although not as often found on decks as stain or natural finish, can be the great equalizer, unifying house, deck, and out buildings.

Select furnishings that support the dominant design. Use small elements to bring contrasts of color, shape, or texture. Gardens, edgings, walls, stone, tiles, bricks, logs, gates, furnishings, lights, and decorative pieces—all add pleasing and lively accents.

PAINT A PATTERN

Alternate decking patterns can add unusual appeal to your deck—and about a third more to your budget. Paint—or better yet, stain—a pattern on your deck. A penetrating stain won't wear off as quickly as a deck paint, and as the wood weathers so will the stain, adding to its antique charm. Score the pattern lines to keep the stain from bleeding across the squares.

LET THE LINES LEAD THE EYE

Vertical lines in tongue and grooved siding lead the eye down to the the first platform. From there, the horizontal lines take over and ease you out into the landscape.

LOOK OUT ON AN OASIS

Decks can be a vantage point for stunning views, those created either by nature or a gardener. High walls can provide privacy to a master bedroom, but strategically lowering them opens up the view where privacy is no longer needed. Use color and material choices to unify your deck, not only with the house, but with the surrounding garden.

PICKING UP THE PATTERNS

Most decks look rustic because they're made of wood. But a deck can also fit right into a contemporary setting. This house's strong horizontal siding lines are mirrored with horizontal fascia and horizontal railings. The railing sections themselves, conforming to the lengths of the cascading platforms, break up the straight lines. Shrubs and bushes hide the structure under the deck.

WOOD IN THE WOODS

Decks are easily integrated into woodland surroundings, and an innovative deck design can enhance the setting. Flower boxes on this deck bring color to the forest backdrop, an enticing accent for the rustic setting. Instead of vertical balusters, the railing is built with solid panels and massive hand-made lattice sections that balance the tall, straight tree trunks.

SEATING WITH STYLE

After railings, built-in seating can function as the next most prominent architectural feature of your deck. Railings usually are not required on a ground-level platform deck, but that's no reason to exclude them. This double-duty seating increases the usefulness of the deck and helps define its boundary.

AN ECLECTIC OVERHEAD DESIGN

Overhead structures usually only have to support themselves, which can give you more design latitude than a railing or decking pattern. Eclectic designs are more easily integrated into detached decks than those attached to a house.

Many lots do not have the proportions that lend themselves to deck construction. Narrow properties, shallow yards, steep slopes, or undesirable views may make building a deck seem all but impossible. Don't despair, because if you look for them, design opportunities are almost always concealed inside a problem.

Often, a deck can cover unusable outdoor space, such as a steep slope or small side yard, adding a comfortable and functional feature to your house.

Solutions to serious site problems may require a professional designer or licensed contractor. But even if you have to call in the pros, it's good to have a preliminary idea of what you want to do with your deck space. That way, the designer can base a proposal on the limitations of the site and also the needs of your family.

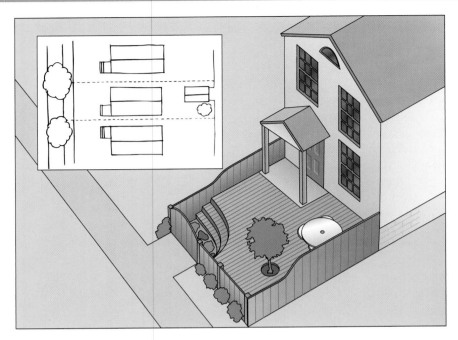

USE ALL OF A NARROW LOT.

Decks for narrow lots with close neighbors often are only as wide as the house. Here, a deck completely fills a narrow city lot, putting a limited front yard to good use. High screens wrapping the structure keep the deck area private and buffer unwanted street noise.

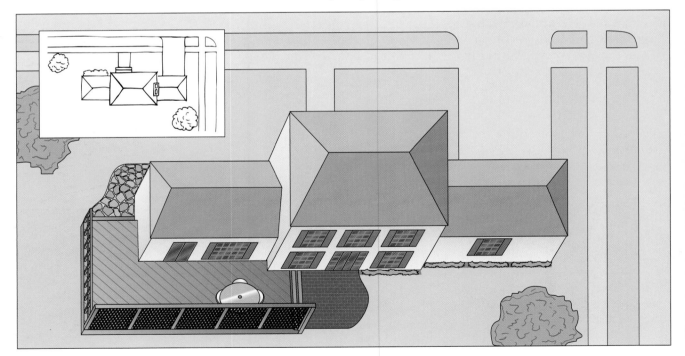

BUILD LONG AND NARROW ON A SHALLOW LOT.

A lot that doesn't lend itself to an expansive deck shouldn't stop you from building one. A long, narrow deck, say 8×30 feet, might just fit the bill. This example wraps around the corner of the house and includes a new stone walk that connects it to the front of the house.

The design centers on a sliding door for access to the family room and includes lattice panels to screen the deck from the street. A patio extends the usable space while adding an extra level.

BLOCK AN UNSIGHTLY VIEW.

The edges of a neighboring yard often become a storage area for the unused items people just can't part with. This unsightly stuff may be invisible from your neighbor's point of view, but right up against what you want to use for outdoor living space. Since the neighbor is not likely to move his storage space, you'll have to make the adjustment by building screening.

This deck not only includes an attached privacy fence, its orientation and seating direct the views and traffic flow away from the lot next door.

TAKE ADVANTAGE OF A STEEP SLOPE.

Steep slopes can be both an advantage and disadvantage. Because the ground drops quickly away from the house, a deck on a steep slope can offer spectacular, sweeping views. But this kind of deck can be more difficult to build. Whether the ground slopes down or up from the deck site, a multilevel deck that follows the contour of the landscape is often the best solution.

▼ CAUTION

CONSULT LOCAL CODES

Elevated decks on steep slopes may require well-engineered foundations and framing. You may need to assess soil integrity, drainage, and earthquake vulnerability. Before building on a steep slope, check with your building officials; you might need to consult a landscape architect or engineer.

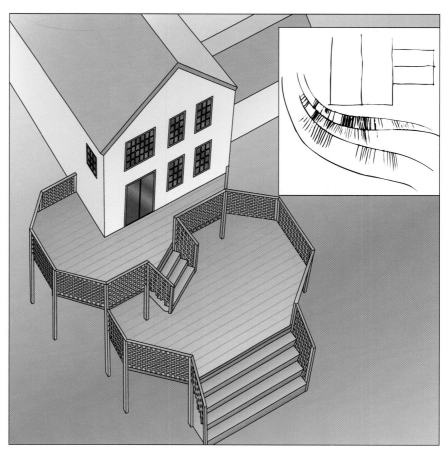

NEW LIFE FOR OLD DECKS

If you have an impractical existing deck, don't tear it down and start over. Try enhancing it, instead.

If the deck is larger than you need, divide it into smaller, more useable spaces with raised planters or moveable seating.

If your deck is too small for the large gatherings you would like to have, build a detached deck and link the new space to the old with a boardwalk. Installing a brick patio at the bottom of the old deck will also increase living space. Often, just a small platform, built from the same lumber as the old deck, will fix the problem. Finish the new material so it blends in with the old.

Open up the views to make the deck seem larger. Remove tall hedges you don't need for privacy.

Brighten up the view. Gather all the unsightly utilitarian items—garbage cans, compost bins, and loose yard tools—into a single service area next to the air conditioner or heating equipment. Build an attractive screen to hide them and make the view more pleasant.

If you feel you're on display while meditating on the deck, shield the area with a fence or shrubs. If the visual intrusion comes from a second story, add an overhead structure.

Whatever you do, build on what you have. Instead of trying to jam a fire-pit into a deck that's already cramped, extend the deck out into the yard to accommodate this new amenity. Fasten decking to sleepers anchored to an old slab patio. You'll be amazed at the magic that results.

CLEAR A PATH
If your deck is underused, maybe all it needs is a little rearranging. Furnishings in the middle of a natural pathway take an area out of service. Move them to the sides of the deck, leaving the central area open.

PREPARING FOR THE PROJECT

The transition from theory to practice can be the most difficult phase of a deck-building project. This is where questions may start to concern you.
- Will the deck be big enough?
- Does it fit the budget?
- Do I have the skills needed to build it?

Listen carefully to the questions and try to answer them thoroughly before proceeding. Don't rush into the project; think through all of the consequences and procedures. If you've just recently moved into the house, it might be too soon to build a deck. By waiting a full year, you will give yourself time to observe the house through a full course of seasonal changes and weather conditions.

Budgeting is a tricky—and highly personal—part of the project. With thorough planning, however, you can avoid surprises. As long as you are supplying all of the labor, you can determine your expenses by preparing a detailed list of materials (drawn from your equally detailed plans), and can take it to several suppliers for estimates. Only you can decide if you want to borrow the money and build today, or save the money and build tomorrow.

Deck building is straightforward work, but parts of it are physically demanding and all of it requires close attention to detail. If you are still concerned about your own ability to build the deck you want, try to narrow down those parts of the job that most trouble you. Perhaps you worry about getting the ledger installed correctly and the posts set nice and straight. If so, act as a general contractor and subcontract parts of the job. You may be able to hire an experienced carpenter to work with you on all or part of the job. This mini-apprenticeship may be all you need to boost your confidence for the next remodeling project.

While you are getting ready to start, call your utilities and have them mark underground lines in your yard. This will show you where it's safe to dig holes for footings.

No matter how long it takes, resolve your doubts before ordering lumber. When the lumber truck backs into your yard, you should have a building permit in hand, a clear idea of what your deck will look like, and a plan for who's going to do the work.

PLAY IT SAFE

Things that make decks interesting–stairways, railings, hot tubs, high elevations–create safety hazards, especially for children. Compliance with local codes and zoning restrictions won't guarantee you the safest deck. These requirements represent minimal standards; your particular situation may demand more. Minimize the risk with a few simple precautions:

■ When building a deck railing, space the balusters no more than 4 inches apart, even if your local code allows wider spacing.
■ Treat deck stairs as you do indoor stairs; if young children are around, put a gate at the top. Put another one at the bottom if the stairs lead to a part of to the house or another area you don't want the child to enter.
■ If you install built-in benches, make the railings behind them at least 24 inches above the seat to prevent a child from climbing or tipping over the side.
■ Before you design railings with horizontal infill, such as piping, check with your building department officials. Codes may prohibit them because children can use them as a ladder to climb over the railing.
■ Fence off a hot tub or spa, and install a childproof gate. If that's not practical, use a secure cover.

MAKE A CONSTRUCTION SCHEDULE

Now is the time to make a construction schedule to keep track of all the tasks you have to complete. Each list will be different, but most will include these steps:

■ Finalize materials list, costs
■ Conduct site analysis
■ Draw plans and elevations
■ Apply for building permit
■ Modify plan as necessary and schedule inspections
■ Order materials
■ Strip sod and prepare site
■ Attach ledger
■ Set batterboards, lay out site
■ Dig footings, set posts
■ Hang beams and joists
■ Fasten decking
■ Build railings and stairs
■ Apply deck finish

PREVENT ROT AND WATER DAMAGE

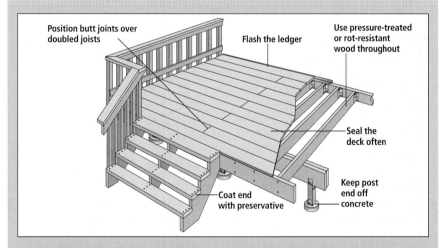

Position butt joints over doubled joists

Flash the ledger

Use pressure-treated or rot-resistant wood throughout

Seal the deck often

Coat end with preservative

Keep post end off concrete

Rot can reduce a deck to ruin. Rot-producing fungi thrive in wood that always stays moist. Here are some ways to protect your deck from moisture:
■ Set posts in metal brackets, so they won't make contact with the earth or concrete.
■ A built-up beam (a beam using two separate boards) lasts longer if you use moisture-draining spacers (see page 46).

■ Incorporate butt joints into the decking so that water can drain. Position the joints over doubled joists with spacers between them to provide a path for water to drain.
■ Pay attention to flashing around the ledger.
■ Brush extra preservative on all cut ends of pressure-treated lumber, especially the ends of support and railing posts.

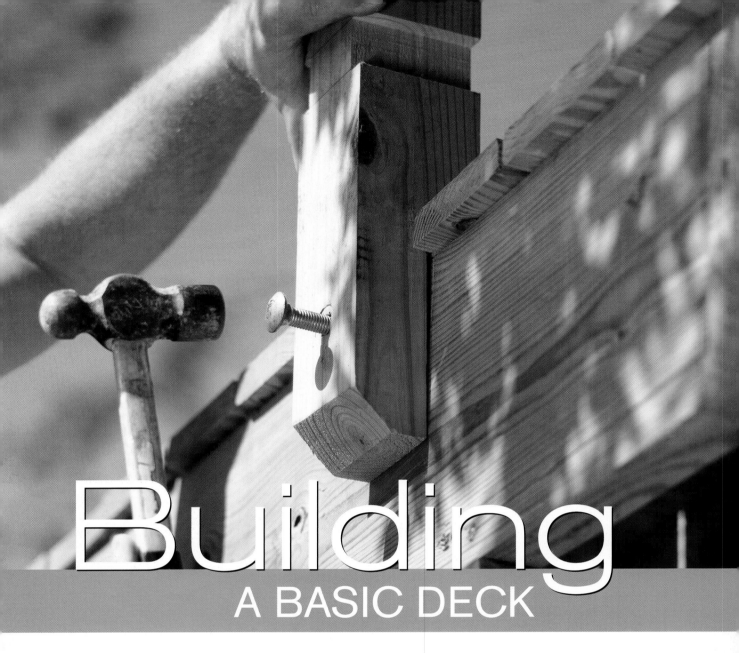

Building
A BASIC DECK

The title above might seem to imply that there's only one way to build a deck; actually, there is one basic set of procedures and techniques. A basic deck will vary with the materials available in your region, the tools you have on hand, the skills you possess, and perhaps most importantly, local building codes. The simple and reliable techniques in this chapter have been used for many years. They will produce a strong, safe, and professional-looking structure that meets building codes in most areas. To be sure, take your plans to your building department before you build; codes are constantly evolving. When your plans are approved, make a list of prospective helpers. You can build a deck singlehandedly, but it's a lot more fun and less tiring if your have some helpers. A 12-foot deck beam is heavy and easier to set and steady with extra pairs of hands. If you're new to home improvement, pick a couple of friends who have experience. Most people are glad to share their knowledge and lend a hand.

PACE YOURSELF

Decks are best built in stages. Before you begin any work, plan a realistic work schedule that spans several weekends, if necessary. Most accidents occur when the work is rushed or the worker is tired. Include breaks in your work schedule. Building a deck is an orderly process; finish one task before you start the next. By the time you reach the stage shown here—installing the railings—your work is nearly complete.

PRECISION COUNTS

Deck construction requires a fairly high level of precision. Don't count on the measurements in your dimensioned plan to be perfect every time. Measure every piece on site before cutting and installing it.

SAFETY FIRST

Power tools are great labor-saving devices, but they can be dangerous. Wear safety glasses, ear protection, and a dust mask when sawing or using any tool which produces dust. Hard-soled work boots and knee pads are a plus. And don't leave tools on top of a ladder. When you move the ladder, you'll receive a hard reminder of where you left them.

DRAWING PLANS

All you need to make accurate deck plans are a pencil, ruler, and graph paper. A dimensioned plan that's drawn to scale will help when you order materials, calculate costs, and keep your construction on schedule. You'll probably also need a plan to submit to the building department for approval.

Draw your deck to scale on graph paper (typically ¼ inch to the foot). You'll need at least a site plan, a plan view, and one or two elevations. You may also want to draw detailed plans for complex parts of the deck. Drawing plans can be tedious, but it's worth the effort to make the project go smoothly.

TAKE MEASUREMENTS.

Deck plans begin with measurements of your property. Take a 100-foot tape (and a pad and pencil) out in your yard and measure the distance from the house to the property lines, the dimensions of the house, the location of windows and doors, electrical outlets, dryer vents, and water valves.

DRAW A SITE PLAN.

A site plan is a drawing that shows your property boundaries, the house, and other major features. It also shows the distances between elements in your landscape that might affect the construction of your deck. A simple deck plan only needs to be a sketch that includes these measurements. More complicated deck plans will require a scaled drawing.

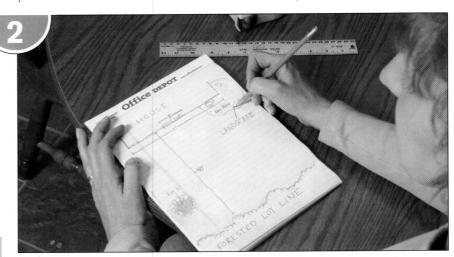

DRAFTING TOOLBOX

You can draw a deck plan quickly with these tools.

- A pad of graph paper (use a ¼-inch grid) and tracing paper
- Drafting tape (to hold the paper down)
- Two or three #3 pencils (the harder lead makes more precise lines than #2s)
- A good eraser
- A 12-inch ruler, circle templates, and perhaps an architect's scale

MAKE DETAILED PLANS.

With detailed plans that show every framing member, you can count the pieces of lumber you need. You can also show obstacles such as dryer vents; plans will help you work around them. Detailed plans can also save you money. For example, because lumber is sold in even lengths, you can keep costs down by making deck dimensions correspond to these lengths. If your detailed plan specifies a 12½-foot ledger and you can reduce the size to 12 feet, you'll avoid cutting a 14-foot board and wasting a lot of lumber.

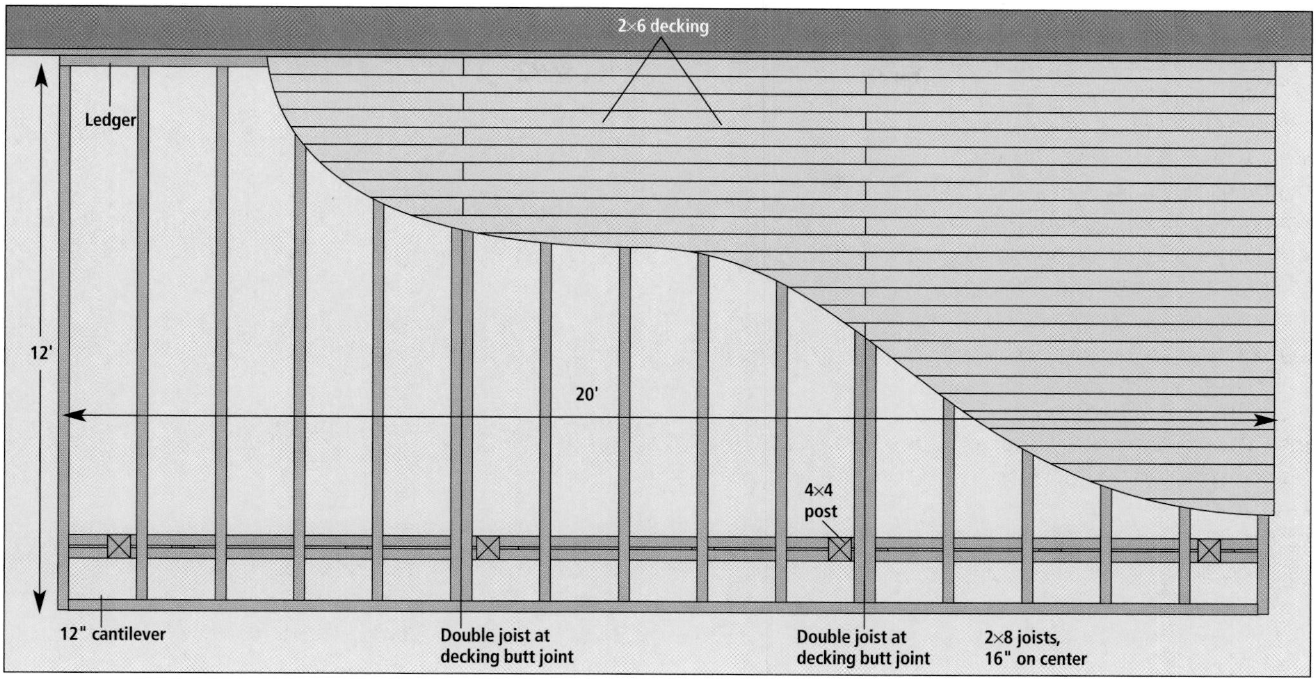

COMPLETE A PLAN (OVERHEAD) VIEW.

A plan view shows the deck as viewed from above. It illustrates the exact location of piers, beams, and joists. It may also include a partial view of the decking, railing, and any other structures attached to the deck.

The drawing above combines a view of the framing with the decking installed above the beams and posts. For more complex decks, these two views can be drawn separately. Draw the foundation and framing plan first, then use tracing paper to produce the finished view.

Include all dimensions—overall length and width, joist and beam spacing, and material sizes.

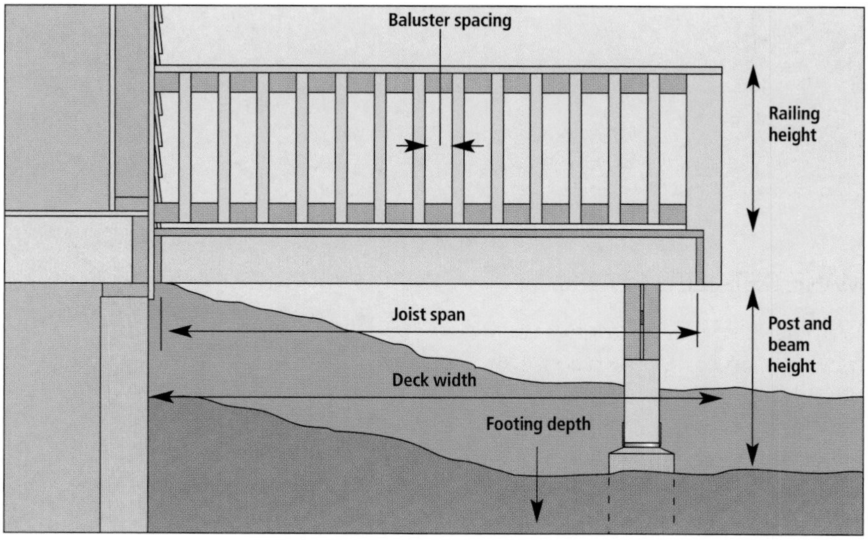

ELEMENTS OF AN ELEVATION (SIDE OR FRONT) VIEW.

A front or side elevation illustrates the vertical arrangement of deck elements—footings, posts, railings, and any built-in planters, benches, or overhead structures. Each elevation should show the depth of the footings, spans, and post and railing dimensions. Railing dimensions should indicate the height of the railing as well as baluster spacing.

COMPUTER ASSISTED PLANNING

Design your deck with computer assisted drafting (CAD) software. Most CAD versions will produce a plan view, an elevation, and a perspective. Many will also produce a list of lumber and materials.

If you're not confident of your computer skills, ask your home center staff for help. Many retail outlets offer computer planning programs and have staff members who know how to use them. Bring in a rough drawing with dimensions (height, width, and length) and have the computer draw your plans.

If your deck will be attached to your house, installing a ledger is the first step in laying out the site. (Free-standing decks are supported on all sides by posts and footings.)

A ledger is a header that's attached to the house. A ledger transfers the weight of the deck to the framing and foundation of the house. That's why the fasteners on a frame house (usually lag screws, but sometimes bolts) must penetrate the sheathing and anchor firmly into the band joist or studs. On brick, block, or concrete construction, use masonry anchors or studs in holes drilled into the masonry.

Installing a ledger usually requires removing the siding so the ledger can rest against a flat surface. Cut metal siding with a circular saw and metal-cutting blade. Cut vinyl and wood siding with a circular saw and a carbide-tipped blade.

Be careful when cutting your ledger. Use the same size stock as the joists. Cut the ledger 3 inches shorter than the width of the framing to allow a 1½-inch space at each end of the ledger for attaching the rim joists.

Using a ledger can also reduce your costs and labor—you have fewer postholes to dig so you have less concrete to pour.

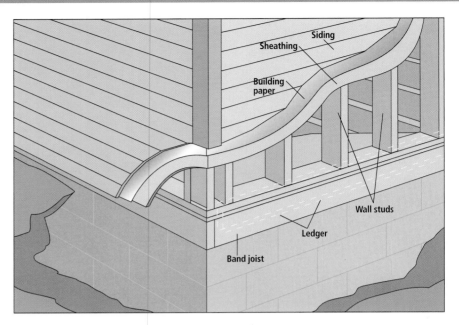

LOCATE THE LEDGER ON THE HOUSE.

The framing and foundation of your house provide several secure points for anchoring the ledger. The actual placement of the ledger will depend on your deck design and the location of the door which provides access to it. Most decks are first-floor structures and anchor into the band joist. Other deck designs will require that you drive the fasteners into the studs or into the masonry foundation.

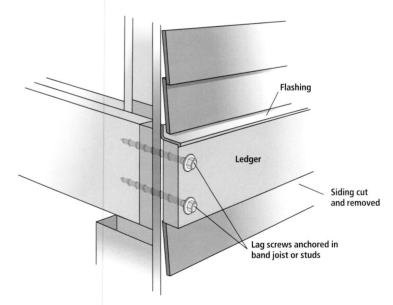

LEDGER ON SIDING.

Wherever you put the ledger—if your house is sided with wood, metal, or vinyl siding—a section of the siding has to come off. Installing the ledger on top of the siding will crush the siding, leaving the ledger in incomplete contact with the surface behind it. That could cause the ledger to fail. Ledgers also need flashing (preformed or flat metal stock), which slides under the siding and extends over the ledger to keep water from collecting behind it.

1

MARK THE TOP EDGE OF THE LEDGER.

Decking should sit from 1 to 3 inches below the bottom of the threshold. Add this space to the thickness of the decking and make a mark for the top of the ledger. For 2×6 decking installed 3 inches below the door, your mark would fall 4½ inches below the bottom of the threshold.

2

MARK THE LEDGER LENGTH.

Set one end of a water level on your mark and the other at a point longer than the length of the ledger. Mark one side and the other with the same method. Snap a chalk line between the marks. Add 1½ inches to the length of the ledger and mark this length on your chalk line.

3

CHECK FOR LEVEL.

At both ends of the ledger marks, measure down from the top line an amount equal to the width of the ledger. Snap chalk lines between the marks or use a level or straightedge to connect the marks on short ledgers. Check your lines for level at various points and adjust them if necessary.

LAG SCREWS OR BOLTS?

You can bolt the ledger to the band joist, but you need to reach the back to put on the nut. Lag screws are easier to install and make a strong connection. Use carriage bolts for bolted joints when the head will be visible; hex-head machine bolts when looks don't matter.

CAUTION

LEDGERS AND LADDERS

Installing a ledger for a first-floor deck won't pose a serious safety problem. But for a second-story deck, you will have to work on a ladder. Ledgers can be heavy and throw you off balance. Use braces (page 30) or get some help. Drive stakes against the bottom of the ladder legs to keep it from slipping on a slope.

Installing a ledger on siding *(continued)*

4 MARK JOIST LOCATIONS.

Layout square marks the outline of the joists—¾" on either side of the center line

Mark the joist spacing (usually 12 or 16 inches on center) on the ledger, allowing for the rim joists to be attached to the ends of the ledger. For 16-inch centers, make the mark for the edge of the first interior joist 15¼ inches from the end of the ledger. Transfer the marks to the ledger face.

5 CUT SIDING AND FLASH.

Set your circular saw depth to the thickness of the siding and cut along the ledger outline. Cut flashing to the length of the cutout and slide it at least 1 inch under the siding above the cutout. Pressure will hold it in place. Overlap flashing joints by 3 inches and notch it for the doorway.

6 LEVEL THE LEDGER.

Hoist the ledger in place and center it in the cutout, leaving 1½ inches on either side for the rim joists. Tack one end of the ledger to the sheathing with one 10d nail or deck screw. Level the ledger and tack the other end. Don't fasten it just yet.

FINISHING THE CUTS

A circular saw can't cut into the corners on the siding. Chisel out the corners on wood siding with a sharp wood chisel. Cut metal and vinyl siding corners with metal snips.

USE BRACES WHEN WORKING ALONE

If you're working by yourself, putting the ledger into its exact position and getting it to stay there can be almost impossible unless you use braces.

Cut 2x4 braces a little longer than the height of the ledger and notch one end if you want. Prop the braces at an angle below both ends of the ledger cutout. Then lift the ledger and set it on the braces—one at a time, if necessary.

Keeping the face of the ledger flat against the sheathing, slide the ledger so it's centered in the opening, leaving 1½ inches on each side for the end joists. Adjust the brace on one end with one hand (don't let go of the ledger), until the top of the ledger rests on the top of

the cutout. Tack this end to the sheathing with a 10d nail or deck screw. Pivot the ledger on this fastener, level the board by adjusting the brace at the other end of the ledger, and tack that end of the ledger.

For ledgers fastened to studs, space fasteners at house stud spacing

Keep fasteners about 2 inches from top and bottom edge

7 MARK FOR FASTENERS.

Beginning about 2 inches from one end, mark fastener locations at 18-to 24-inch intervals. Mark both the top and bottom edge of the ledger, using a layout square. Don't worry if a fastener is at a deck joist location.

8 DRILL PILOT HOLES.

Counterbore lag-screw locations that fall on deck joist markings, then drill pilot holes for the lag screws through the ledger and about ¾ inch into the band joist or studs. Drive washered lag screws with a socket wrench.

9 SEAL THE EDGES.

Let the ledger settle overnight, then tighten the screws again, stopping when they won't turn without force. Caulk the counterbores, the top of the flashing, and the bottom of the ledger with exterior silicone caulk.

INSTALLING A LEDGER ON STUCCO

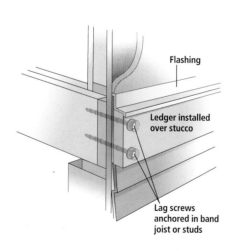

Flashing

Ledger installed over stucco

Lag screws anchored in band joist or studs

STUCCO SIDING.

Stucco acts essentially as a layer of siding (one that consists of concrete), so fastening a ledger to stucco involves the same techniques as for wood or vinyl siding. Stucco doesn't have to be removed, but does require a groove for anchoring the flashing.

1 CUT A GROOVE.

Hang the ledger on the stucco. Mark the wall about an inch above the ledger and tack a guide on the ledger so the saw blade will cut on the mark. Using a circular saw with a masonry blade, cut a ¼-inch-deep kerf from one end of the ledger to the other.

2 SEAL THE FLASHING.

Blow the dust out of the kerf with a compressed air can, then push the lip of the flashing into the kerf until it's seated firmly. Then seal the top of the flashing with silicone caulk.

A ledger on a brick, block, or poured concrete wall has to be anchored to the masonry material because there's no framing to support it. It must be securely fastened so it can withstand the downward pressure of the deck.

The beam and perimeter posts bear about half of the load of the deck away from the house. The ledger must support the rest of the weight.

You can secure the ledger to the masonry with epoxied threaded studs (as shown at right), with lag shields and lag screws, or with masonry bolts in poured concrete. If you epoxy threaded studs into the masonry, use epoxy made for that purpose. Lag shields are made to be used with lag bolts. Don't use any other masonry anchor. Although most of the stress put on ledger anchors will be down (not out), inadequate anchors could let the deck work loose and pull away from the wall.

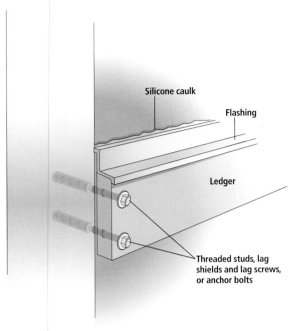

Silicone caulk

Flashing

Ledger

Threaded studs, lag shields and lag screws, or anchor bolts

LEDGER ON MASONRY.

There are two kinds of threaded studs, short precut lengths for use in masonry installations and continuous threaded lengths (up to 4 feet) called all-thread. Cutting all-thread to length often results in damaged or distorted threads and uneven lengths.

Precut studs are easier to use. Use studs with a diameter of at least $3/8$ inch; $1/2$-inch studs are better. When fastening a ledger to concrete block, be sure the fasteners enter the webs (the solid part) of the block, not the cores (the open voids).

1 OUTLINE THE LEDGER.

Mark the wall so the top edge of the ledger will be at the correct point below the threshold. For short ledgers, extend the mark with a level. Use a water level over long spans. Mark the length of the ledger and snap a line between the marks.

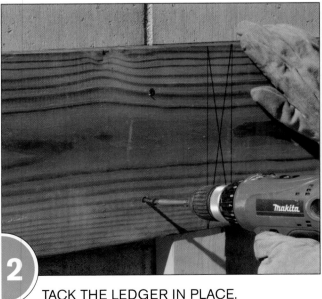

2 TACK THE LEDGER IN PLACE.

Mark the ledger for both joist and fastener locations. Then tack the ledger to the masonry with concrete screws, making sure the ledger is level with your chalk line. Brace the ledger against the wall if necessary.

3 DRILL MARKER HOLES.

Mark a twist drill just short of 1½ inches and drill marker holes at your fastener locations. Don't push past the mark on the drill bit or you'll ruin the tip of the twist drill.

4 DRILL ANCHOR HOLES.

Insert a masonry bit of the same size in a hammer drill and drill the fastener holes 3 inches into the masonry. The hammer drill will push through the undrilled wood at the bottom of the marker hole.

5 EPOXY THE HOLES.

Remove the ledger if you prefer. Prepare the epoxy syringe, making sure both its parts will mix evenly. Insert the syringe in the hole and push out the epoxy—only into the masonry, not the ledger.

6 INSERT STUDS.

Insert a threaded stud into each hole right after you've epoxied it. If you wait until all the holes are epoxied, the glue may set up, so you might not be able to get the studs into the first holes. Square the studs to the ledger (or to the wall if you've removed the ledger) with a layout square.

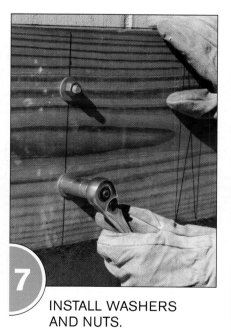

7 INSTALL WASHERS AND NUTS.

Let the epoxy cure overnight and replace the ledger over the studs if you previously removed it. Slide washers over the studs and tighten the nuts with a socket wrench. Don't overtighten—stop when the washer begins to dent the wood.

USING LAG SCREWS

To use lag screws, you'll need lag shields. Tack (or brace) the ledger in place and drill marker holes, then mark the wall with a small masonry bit. Remove the ledger and use a larger masonry bit to drill holes for the lag shields. Tap the shields flush with the wall and hang the ledger with the lag screws.

PREPARING THE SITE

Most deck sites require some preparation so the ground under the deck will drain properly and won't become filled with weeds. You can prepare the site after laying out the batterboards, but removing the sod first will make the layout easier.

Then, eliminate any drainage problems, especially around the foundation. Beginning at the foundation and out to about 4 feet, slope the soil away from the house. If a downspout empties on the deck site, reroute it. Divert water that will flow off the deck with a drainage ditch around the perimeter.

1 **STAKE THE CORNERS.**

Drive a temporary stake (or a batterboard) near the house about where the corner of the deck will be (or just outside the corner). Using your scaled plan, measure and stake the other three corners. You don't need to be exact; you'll fine-tune the outline later.

2 **RUN LINES.**

Run mason's between the stakes a couple of inches above the ground. Measure the diagonals and adjust the stakes until the diagonals are equal. Tighten the lines and spray-paint or chalk the footprint on the grass.

YOU'LL NEED

TIME: About one hour to run lines; more to remove sod and lay fabric

SKILLS: Measuring, digging

TOOLS: Shovel, rake, hammer, small sledge, mason's line

3 **REMOVE THE SOD AND SOIL.**

Remove the lines and slice the sod in strips with a spade. Dislodge the roots with a spade and roll up the sod. Leave the stakes in place. Excavate the site to a 2-inch depth.

Lay gravel before or after digging post holes

4 **LAY FABRIC AND GRAVEL.**

Lay landscape fabric (weed block) in the excavation from edge to edge, overlapping the seams by 6 to 12 inches. Pour in crushed stone and rake it level with a garden rake.

LAYING OUT A DECK

aying out a deck site—marking the perimeter of the deck with mason's lines and locating the footings—isn't hard work, but it does require some precision. It doesn't have to be perfect because you can still make minor adjustments when you set the posts, but the success of your project depends on aligning the centers of the footings. Although laying out the site won't wear you out, you can do it much more quickly and

accurately with someone to help pull lines tight, hold the loose end of the measuring tape, adjust lines, and double-check the layout for errors.

You'll need a pair of batterboards (page 36) at each corner. If you can't drive them close to the house, substitute a stake or 1× board tacked to the siding . Mason's lines tied to batterboards allow you to square the corners and make straight lines for centering the line footings for the posts between the corners.

The illustration below shows a typical site layout and its relationship to the finished deck. All mason's lines run through the center of the footings. The next two pages illustrate layout steps for a freestanding deck. If you've already fastened a ledger to the house for an attached deck, start with the steps in the box on the bottom of page 37, then follow the remaining steps to complete your layout.

(page 36)

bottom of page 37

YOU'LL NEED

TIME: About six hours for a 12×16-foot deck

SKILLS: Measuring, leveling, making simple calculations

TOOLS: Tape measure, cordless drill, small sledge, plumb bob, mason's line, line level, wooden stakes

CAUTION

EDGES OR CENTERS?

You can lay out your deck site with the mason's lines set to mark either the edges of the posts or their centers. If the lines mark the post edges, you'll have to move them at some time by half the thickness of the post. This method is effective if you don't get the two mixed up. If one line marks the centers and another the edges of the posts, your whole layout will be off.

After laying out the deck, set up a work site close by, but out of the way.

And before you dig postholes, have your utilities survey the area to mark underground lines.

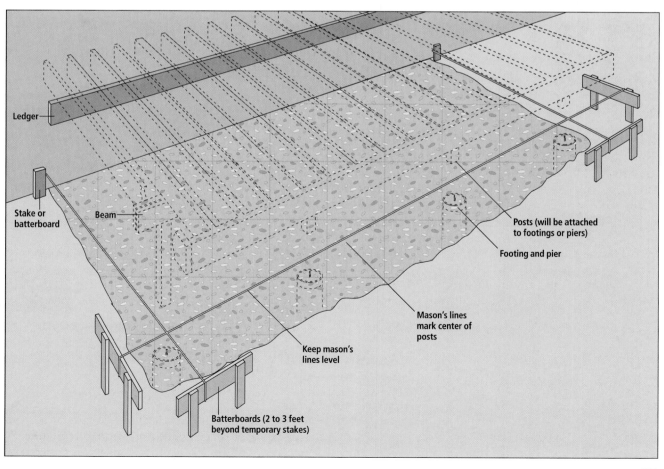

Ledger

Stake or batterboard

Beam

Posts (will be attached to footings or piers)

Footing and pier

Mason's lines mark center of posts

Keep mason's lines level

Batterboards (2 to 3 feet beyond temporary stakes)

Laying out a deck *(continued)*

BUILD BATTERBOARDS.

Make batterboards from 2- to 3-foot pointed 2×4 legs and an 18- to 36-inch 1×4 crosspiece. You might need batterboards with longer legs on a sloped site. Many lumberyards and home centers sell pointed stakes, or you can cut points on the stakes yourself. Cut the crosspiece to length and attach it to the stakes with 1½-inch screws. Place the batterboards at right angles to each other and 2 to 3 feet beyond your temporary corner stakes. If you use a stake at the house, center it in line with the center of your corner post. Drive the stakes deep enough to support tightly stretched lines. The crosspieces should be up about 18 to 24 inches above grade.

1

1×4 crosspiece

2×4 legs

Stake or batterboard at house

Level mason's lines with a line level

Mason's line tied at center of post

2

STRING MASON'S LINES.

Stringing and adjusting mason's lines is easier with two people. Mark the siding for the edge of the decking then for the center of the corner post. The post is usually placed inside the decking line a distance equal to the amount of overhang plus the thickness of the end joist plus ½ the thickness of the post. Tie a line to the crosspiece (or stake) at this point and to the crosspiece of the corner batterboard. Keep it roughly square to the house. Do the same on the opposite side of the deck. Next, tie a mason's line parallel to the house and lined up with the center of the line footings. Pull the lines tight and level them by driving in the batterboards. Make sure the lines touch where they intersect.

3 SQUARE THE LAYOUT.

To square the layout, use any even multiple of a 3-4-5 triangle. The larger the numbers, the greater the accuracy. In this case, measure 6 feet along one line and mark the spot with a piece of tape. Measure 8 feet along the perpendicular line or on the siding and mark it also. Measure the distance between the two marks. If it is exactly 10 feet, the lines are square. If not, adjust one line. Square each corner with the same method.

4 MARK THE CROSSPIECE.

Once you've squared the layout, mark the position of the line on each crosspiece. If the lines get bumped or when you need to take them down and restring them, you can reset them to the marks to maintain the layout.

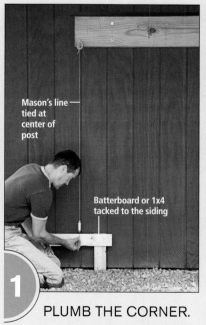

5 MARK FOOTINGS.

To mark the center of a corner footing, hold a plumb line barely touching the intersection of the lines. Drive a stake or landscape spike into the ground to mark the spot below the plumb bob. If your design includes line posts between the corners, measure along the line and use a plumb bob to mark the center of the footings. Mark an X across each stake or spike with chalk or spray paint.

LAYING OUT WITH A LEDGER

Mason's line — tied at center of post

Batterboard or 1x4 tacked to the siding

1 PLUMB THE CORNER.

Drive a nail into the ledger at the center line of the post (Step 2, page 36). Drop a plumb line from the nail to the batterboard (or 1x4).

2 TIE LINE TO BATTERBOARD.

Let the plumb bob come to rest. Then hold a scrap 1x just touching the plumb line and mark the crosspiece where the scrap intersects it. Tie a mason's line at this mark and continue your layout, following the procedure that begins in Step 2 on the opposite page.

DIGGING FOOTINGS

Before you dig footings, ask your local building department for specific requirements for type, depth, and strength of posts and footings. Footings need to be stable in soft soil, withstand frost, and provide a base that keeps posts or beams above moisture. See page 40 for more information on footing options. Also have your utilities survey the area to locate underground lines.

In cold climates, footings should extend below the frost line (the depth to which frost penetrates the soil. This prevents the deck structure from rising and falling during freeze-thaw cycles.

Frost depth is not the only thing that affects the depth of the footing. Soil composition, the size of the post, and the height of the deck also affect footing depth.

Don't dig post holes with a shovel; borrow, rent, or buy a clamshell digger. A clamshell digger is an efficient tool for digging a few holes by hand, better than the old-style hand auger. If your design requires a large number of footings, rent a power auger (see page 117) or hire a professional. If you rent a power auger, be sure to get instructions on its use. If you will pile removed soil on a grassy area, lay a sheet of plywood or plastic first.

(see page 117)

YOU'LL NEED

TIME: One to four hours, depending on the digging tool, the type of soil, and the number and depth of the holes

SKILLS: Using a manual post-hole digger requires no special skills, but get instructions before using a power auger

TOOLS: Garden spade, clamshell posthole digger, digging bar, plywood or plastic sheet, level, handsaw, small sledge

1 START THE FOOTING.

Unstring the mason's lines and spread your feet on both sides of the X that marks the center of the footing. With the handles of the digger parallel to each other, drive the blades into the soil. Let the weight of the digger do as much of the work as possible.

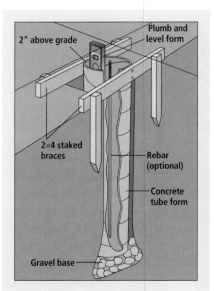

2" above grade — Plumb and level form

2×4 staked braces

Rebar (optional)

Concrete tube form

Gravel base

A TYPICAL FOOTING.

A typical footing installation consists of a concrete tube form set in the hole and plumbed with braced stakes. The hole will probably be a little larger than the tube form, so be sure to center the form before you stake the braces. If codes require rebar, don't put it in the center of the hole—that's where your J-bolt will go.

2 REMOVE THE SOIL.

Pull the handles apart to hold the soil between the blades and lift the digger straight up. Move the digger away from the hole and release the soil by pushing the handles together. At the proper depth, flare the bottom of the hole by angling the blades.

3 POUR A GRAVEL BASE.

Clean out loose soil from the bottom of the hole and pour in 2 to 6 inches of crushed gravel (or the depth required by code). Tamp the gravel with a 2×4 or tamping bar. The gravel lets water drain out the bottom of the footing and helps reduce frost heave.

4 CUT THE TUBE FORM.

Mark the tube form so it will reach the level where the hole flares and extend 2 inches above grade. Cut the form with a handsaw, keeping the saw perpendicular to the form to make a straight cut. If the cut looks awkward, put that end in the bottom of the hole. A straight cut, however, makes the form easier to level.

5 BRACE THE FORM.

Lower the form into the hole and fasten it to 2× braces with short screws. Then drive stakes at both ends of the braces. Fasten one end of each brace to a stake and set a 2-foot level on the form. Raise or lower the brace to level the tube, then screw the braces to the stakes. Set the form as plumb as possible (it doesn't have to be perfect).

6 BACKFILL THE FORM.

Backfill the outside edge of the form with a round-nosed shovel, tamping the soil lightly with a 2×2 after every 4 inches of soil. If the footing is more than 3 inches wider than the tube, tamping may fill the flared recess at the bottom of the hole. In this case, pour the footing first, then backfill.

CAUTION

WATCH YOUR BACK

Digging postholes is hard work. If you need to dig holes that are 3 to 4 feet deep, do not be surprised if each one takes a couple of hours. You may spend a good bit of this time prying out rocks and cutting through roots. Don't try to grind rocks out with a clamshell digger. Pry them from the sides of the hole with a tamping bar.

This work can be tough on the arms and shoulders, and even tougher on the back. Even if you are in relatively good physical shape, it makes sense to take your time and take frequent breaks.

POURING FOOTINGS

If your deck will have corner footings only, preparing premixed bags of concrete in a wheelbarrow is quick and cost-effective. If you're pouring more than six footings, rent a power mixer or order truck-delivered ready-mix from a concrete supplier.

Either move the mixer to each hole or move the concrete in a wheelbarrow. Lay a 2×12 ramp to make the job easier and minimize damage to your lawn. Measure the dry ingredients first (in shovelfuls), mix them in the power mixer or wheelbarrow, then add the water.

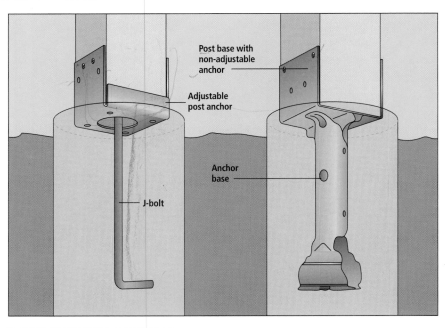

Post base with non-adjustable anchor

Adjustable post anchor

Anchor base

J-bolt

YOU'LL NEED

TIME: About an hour per footing

SKILLS: Basic masonry skills; follow instructions on the bag to mix concrete

TOOLS: Power mixer or wheelbarrow, mason's hoe, shovel, hose, layout square, trowel

POST-ANCHOR OPTIONS.

Post anchors are made in a number of styles, either adjustable or non-adjustable. Non-adjustable anchors are slightly less expensive but require precise setting. Adjustable anchors will give you a margin of error, allowing a correction of up to ½ inch, which makes them worth their slightly higher cost. It's a lot easier to adjust an anchor to center the posts than it is to set the anchor precisely. The installation of footings shown on these pages involves inserting a J-bolt, which is anchored in the concrete and accepts an adjustable anchor.

MIXING IN A WHEELBARROW

Use a large wheelbarrow to minimize spills

Pour in a whole bag (never a partial one) or measure dry ingredients in shovelfuls. Mix the ingredients with a hoe, then mound them and make a depression. Add water in the depression and pull the dry mix into the water, working the mix back and forth and scraping up dry material from the bottom. Add water as necessary.

GETTING THE RIGHT MIX

Whether you're mixing in a wheelbarrow or in a power mixer, make sure all of the ingredients are mixed together thoroughly. To test the consistency of the mix (its slump), scoop up some with a shovel or trowel. When the concrete clings to a shovel or a trowel turned on edge, it's ready.

1 MIX DRY INGREDIENTS.

Bring the mixer or wheelbarrow to the hole. Empty whole pre-mix bags into the mixer or measure cement, sand, and aggregate in shovelfuls. Turn the mixer on to mix the dry materials thoroughly. Then add half the water and mix again. Continue mixing, adding water a little at a time.

2 MAKING THE POUR.

Tip the mixer so the concrete pours straight into the hole. Have a helper guide the flow with a round-nosed shovel. Stop pouring when the hole is half full and consolidate the concrete (see Step 3), then fill the hole. If working from a wheelbarrow, shovel in the concrete.

3 CONSOLIDATE THE MIX.

When the footing is half full (and again when full), consolidate the mix by working a 2×4 up and down in it to remove any air trapped by the pour. Removing air pockets will allow the concrete to cure properly.

4 LEVEL THE FOOTING.

Overfill the form by about 2 inches, then screed off (scrape off and level) the excess with a short length of scrap 2×4. See-saw the screed back and forth to level the mix. Pulling the screed straight back will drag concrete out of the form.

SOAK YOUR PIERS

If you're building a freestanding deck on flat, stable ground where frost heave is not a problem, building codes may allow you to use precast concrete piers instead of footings and posts. If the ground does rise and fall by a small amount, the deck will move as a unit. Because it's not fastened to the house, such movement won't cause the deck to break up.

Some codes require that the piers be bedded in a footing, varying in depth from 1 foot to below the frost line. If your plan calls for bedding precast piers in a footing, be sure to soak the piers in a tub of water for several minutes, then center them in the footing before the concrete sets up. A dry pier will quickly absorb the water from wet concrete, causing it to flake and spall. Such a weakened bond between the pier and concrete could cause the deck structure to fail.

Pouring footings *(continued)*

⑤ SET THE J-BOLT.

Restring the mason's lines to center the J-bolts. When the concrete begins to set (it will resist finger pressure) push a J-bolt into the center of the form, leaving about an inch exposed. Center the bolt with a plumb bob or tape measure.

⑥ SQUARE THE THREADS.

The exposed threads of the J-bolt must be vertical, otherwise the post anchor will not sit squarely on the footing. Square the threads to the footing with a layout square. Repack loose concrete with a pointed trowel, adding a little more if necessary.

INSTALLING A WET-INSERT ANCHOR

① INSERT THE BASE.

Most wet-insert anchors have prongs or a post and must be installed before the concrete sets up. Push the base of the anchor into the center of the footing, rocking it back and forth as you go. Stop when the bottom of the anchor plate touches the footing.

② ALIGN THE ANCHORS.

Line up a long straight 2×4 on the footings, placing it so the edges of all the anchors will be lined up on the same plane. Have someone hold the 2×4 in place while you adjust the position of the anchors.

PREPARING A STAIR LANDING

If you want to build stairs that rest on a concrete pad, you can save time and effort by building forms for the pad and pouring it at the same time as your footings. But you must determine exactly where the pad will be placed, which is difficult to gauge when the deck hasn't been built yet. To accurately position the pad your plans have to be accurate and you have to know where you want the stairs located. See page 56 for information about positioning and building a form for a concrete stair landing.

DRILLING AN ANCHOR BOLT IN CURED CONCRETE

1 DRILL AND EPOXY THE HOLE.

Threaded studs that attach post anchors may be installed after the footings have cured. Hammer drill a hole ⅛ to ³⁄₁₆ inch larger than the stud diameter and deep enough to leave 1 inch exposed. Wrap the top 1 inch of the stud with masking tape. Then blow the dust out of the hole with compressed air. Inject anchor-setting epoxy into the hole and insert the stud immediately.

2 SQUARE THE STUD.

Square the end of the stud to the footing and let the epoxy cure as long as specified by the manufacturer. When the epoxy has cured, measure the height of the threads. If it extends more than 1 inch above the concrete, thread on the nut until its top face is an inch above the concrete. Cut the stud with a hacksaw and remove the nut.

INSTALLING POSTS

When you install the posts, you'll employ the same techniques you used laying out the site—measuring, squaring, and aligning. Only this time, everything needs to line up precisely. That's where adjustable post anchors have an advantage: They will let you correct most alignment problems.

You will work more quickly if you do everything in stages—set all the anchors loosely and line them up, square all the posts, set and brace them in the anchors, then plumb and align all of them.

YOU'LL NEED

TIME: About 45 minutes to anchor and brace each post

SKILLS: Measuring, plumbing, driving fasteners

TOOLS: Hammer, open-end and socket wrenches, drill, tape measure

1 SET THE ANCHORS.

Tighten all the anchors in place just enough so you can move the anchor slightly. On the footings parallel to the house, set a long straight 2×4 across the front edges of the anchors. Line up the anchors so all of them are an equal distance from the house. Then tighten each anchor with a socket wrench. Repeat the process on the side posts, setting up the edge of the anchors closest to the house with a plumb bob.

Installing posts *(continued)*

PREP THE POSTS AND RUN THEM WILD

Plumb posts start out square.
The day before you set the posts, check each of them and square the ends with a layout square and circular or reciprocating saw. Dip the cut ends in preservative and let the preservative soak in overnight.

You can cut the posts to the specified length before you install them, but slight variations in the footings or deck framing might cause some to be too short or too long. Instead, let the lengths of the posts run wild—with each one slightly longer than you need. That way, you can use a water level to mark them at the same height after installation.

2 TACK THE POST BASE.

Set each post in its anchor and drive one nail through the anchor hole and about halfway into the post. Have someone help hold the post as plumb as possible. This will keep the bottom of the post in place but will allow you to move it when you plumb it with braces. Tack a 1×4 brace to the post and stake it. Tack and brace the remaining posts. The posts don't have to be perfectly plumb; you can adjust them in later steps.

3 STAKE THE POSTS.

Move the mason's lines on the crosspiece outside the center line by half the width of the post. Restring the lines and clamp a second 1×4 staked brace to the post. Plumb each post with a post level, keeping its outside face against the mason's line.

4 FASTEN THE POSTS.

Drive the remaining fasteners in the anchors. Some post anchors accept nails or screws only. Others also accept a lag screw. Predrill for the lag screw before driving it.

REDRESSING ANCHOR THREADS

Setting footings and posts can damage the threads of a J-bolt or stud. Protect the threads with tightly wound tape or by turning a nut onto the threads so that it's even with the top of the bolt.

If the threads of an anchor bolt do become damaged, you can clean them up with a hardened steel die, available at your hardware store. Make sure you get one with the same thread. Turn the die on the threads to recut them and clean out any damage. Absent a die, you can often clean up a damaged bolt with a nut. It will suffer some damage in the process, so don't reuse the nut.

MARKING AND CUTTING POSTS

Marking and cutting posts requires patience and precision. Properly cut posts make the rest of the job go easier and will ensure a sturdy, level deck, so don't rush this step. Ask a friend or two to help so you won't have keep moving back and forth from one post to another to adjust them.

If time has passed since you set the posts, check them for plumb and readjust them if necessary.

YOU'LL NEED

TIME: About 30 minutes per post

SKILLS: Measuring, plumbing, cutting, driving fasteners

TOOLS: Framing square, layout square, hammer, post level, wrench, tape measure, carpenter's level, water level, reciprocating saw

1 ESTABLISH THE LEVEL.

Rest one end of a long, straight 2×4 on top of the ledger. Hold the other end against the nearest post. Place a level on top of the 2×4 and level it. Mark the post where the bottom of the 2×4 intersects it. This line is the reference for the next steps.

TOP COAT YOUR POSTS

If you are building your deck with pressure-treated lumber, treat the tops of the posts after you cut them. Although treated wood absorbs preservatives during manufacture, cutting off the end exposes a surface that is less-thoroughly treated. To avoid on-going maintenance problems, brush preservative on the cut ends of the posts. Horizontal surfaces (such as post ends) are most exposed to the weather, but joists and beams need treatment too.

2 MARK THE CUT LINE.

Hold a piece of joist scrap on the reference line and mark the post for the bottom of the joists (top of the beam). Then hold a piece of beam scrap on this second line and mark the bottom of the beam (top of the post). You'll cut the posts along this line.

3 EXTEND THE CUT LINE.

Hold a layout square on an adjacent post face, level with the cut line. Mark this face and the remaining faces. Cut the post on the line with a reciprocating saw. Set one end of a water level against the cut and the other on the next post. Mark all posts with the water level and cut them.

A beam runs parallel to the ledger and supports the joists. There are several ways to construct a beam (see photos, right).

A single 4× or 6× beam reduces construction time, but long pieces may be difficult to find, and are expensive and heavy to handle.

You can build your own beam from doubled lengths of 2× stock. This construction is strong, less expensive, and comes together quickly.

Add ½-inch plywood spacers with mitered tops to a doubled beam to make its width consistent with dimensioned lumber and hardware. The miters on the top of the spacers allow water to drain.

Two lengths of 2× stock sandwiched to the sides of posts, won't be as strong, but may be required because of other factors in your design.

Different deck designs may require you to use a particular method, but local code requirements may determine how you build your beam.

If the beam will rest on top of the posts, strengthen the joint with a post/beam connector.

Use pressure-treated lumber unless you've chosen a naturally rot-resistant wood. Install the beam with its crown side (curved edge) up.

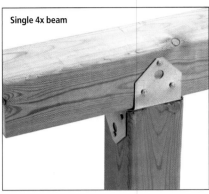

Single 4x beam

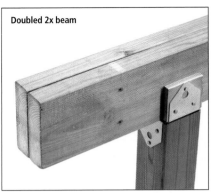

Doubled 2x beam

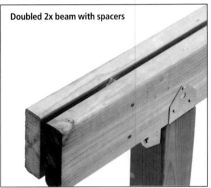

Doubled 2x beam with spacers

Sandwiched beam

YOU'LL NEED

TIME: About three hours for a doubled 16-foot beam, including assembly and installation

SKILLS: Measuring, cutting, fastening, drilling, caulking

TOOLS: Tape measure, hammer, circular saw, drill, socket wrench, level, caulk gun, post level

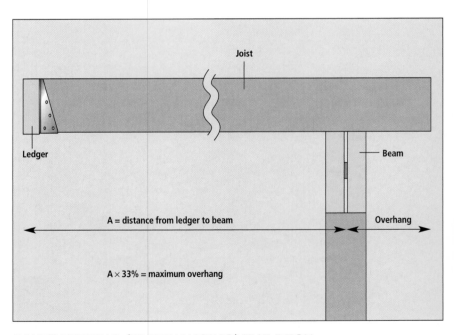

Joist

Ledger

Beam

A = distance from ledger to beam

Overhang

A × 33% = maximum overhang

CANTILEVERING (OVERHANGING) THE DECK.

Cantilevering the front edge of a low deck beyond the beam will make it less visible. It will make a ground-level platform seem to float. Joists can usually overhang the beam up to a third of the total joist length. However, your local building code may set different requirements: Be sure to check cantilever limits. A low deck may be so close to the ground that you won't have room for a large beam. In that case, use smaller beam stock and install an additional post.

SETTING THE BEAM.

Install post/beam connectors on the posts, making sure they're oriented in the same direction. Haul the completed beam assembly to the deck site and lower it into the connectors. Center the beam on the deck site.

BRACING THE BEAM.

Fasten a stake to a 2×4 brace and drive the stake in the ground. With a post level, brace the face of the beam plumb. Install another staked brace on the opposite side and brace it to the posts along its length.

FASTENING THE BEAM.

With the beam braced, attach it to the connectors with screws or nails. Screws are less likely to push the beam out of alignment. Remove the braces when you install the joists.

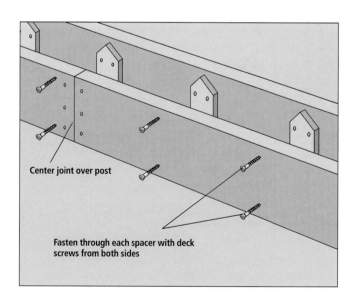

Center joint over post

Fasten through each spacer with deck screws from both sides

BUILDING UP A BEAM.

A doubled 2× beam with ½- or ⅜-inch spacers will match the width of a 4×4 post. Measure the post width—pressure treated posts are sometimes a little thinner than other dimensioned lumber. Point the spacers (pressure-treated plywood) to aid water drainage. Set one board on a solid surface and tack spacers every 24 inches. Set the other member on top and clamp everything together with edges flush. Drive deck screws through each spacer, turn over the beam, then fasten from the other side.

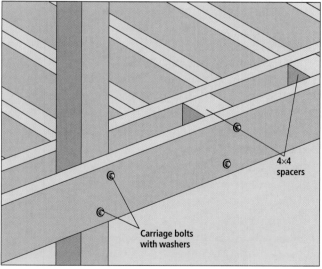

4×4 spacers

Carriage bolts with washers

INSTALLING A SANDWICHED BEAM.

If your deck design requires a 2× sandwiched beam, and the face of the beam will be visible, assemble it with ½-inch carriage bolt. If the beam is not visible, use machine bolts with washers on both ends. Support the beam every 24 inches with spacer blocks cut from post stock. Clamp and level both sides of the beam to the posts before drilling the bolt holes; offset the holes to reduce splitting. Tighten the nuts with a socket wrench.

HANGING JOISTS

No matter how many methods of hanging joists you've heard or read about, you should use joist hangers. Most codes require them, anyway. Unless you plan to clad the header and rim joists with a fascia, select the straightest and least blemished boards for these pieces—and square the ends before measuring.

Fasten the rim joists and header to the ledger and beam, then hang the inner joists. Building this box structure first is easier than hanging the joists first then attaching the header. If you haven't marked joist locations on the ledger and header, do it after you square the frame.

YOU'LL NEED

TIME: Two hours for a 12×16-foot deck, longer if on a ladder

SKILLS: Measuring, cutting, fastening, squaring

TOOLS: Hammer, tape measure, pencil, framing square, layout square, circular saw, cordless drill

CROWN SIDE UP

Dimension lumber often has a slightly bowed edge, or crown. You can see this crowning by sighting down the edge of the board. Crowning is not a structural problem. The weight of the structure will force it level.

1 INSTALL THE RIM JOISTS.

Measure and cut the rim joists to length—usually 1½ inches shorter than the total front-to-back deck dimension. Rest one end of one joist on the beam and fasten the other end flush with the ledger with two 3-inch deck screws. Hang the other rim joist in the same way. You can install angle brackets (page 50) at the ledger joint now or after you square the frame.

2 TACK THE RIM JOIST.

Set a framing square inside the corner at the ledger and again at the intersection of the beam and adjust the rim joists until they are square to the house and the beam. If everything is properly placed, the outer face of the rim joist should be flush with the end of the beam (unless you have a cantilevered design). For now, tack the rim joists to the top of the beam with a toenail or screw.

KEEP IT SQUARE

The more care you take to install the joists square with the ledger, the easier the rest of the construction will be. Don't assume you can square up things later. Use a framing square to align each joist at the header. If your joists are all the same thickness, use a spacer to test their spacing. To make the spacer, cut a perfectly square piece of joist stock exactly 14½ inches long. Have a helper use the scrap to space and align the joists at the beam.

3 INSTALL THE HEADER.

If you have someone to help, one of you should hold the header while the other screws it to the ends of the rim joists. Square the frame with a framing square and check it with a 3-4-5 triangle (see page 120). If necessary, remove the toenails at the beam, adjust the joists, and drive the fasteners in again. Set angle brackets in the corners, if you haven't already. If working alone, prop the header, tack one corner, then the other.

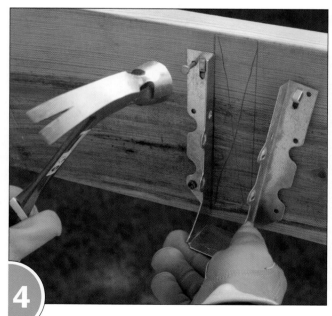

4 MARK THE HANGER LOCATIONS.

Stabilize the frame on the beam with seismic ties (see page 50) and mark joist locations on the ledger and header, if you have not done so already. Make sure the joists are spaced as specified on your dimensioned plan. You can fasten the hangers at the marks as shown here, or using the method described in the next step.

2x flange

5 INSTALL THE JOISTS.

Cut joists to length and tack a 2× flange at each end, extending it 1½ inches past the end. The flange keeps the top of the joist flush with the top of the ledger and header. Set the joist on the marks and slide a joist hanger tight to the bottom. Fasten the hanger to the ledger and header.

Hanging joists *(continued)*

6 FINISH THE INSTALLATION.

Continue fastening hangers, nailing or screwing each joist to the hanger as you go. If the header is bowed, have a helper push it toward the joist while you drive the hanger fasteners.

REINFORCE THE FRAME

Seismic tie

Angle bracket

Framing was once held together by face-nailing or toenailing the joints. Bugle-head (self sinking), coated deck screws make joints easier to fasten, but do not greatly increase the stability of the joint. Framing connectors—such as angle brackets and seismic ties—along with joist hangers greatly increase the strength of framing joints. Most codes require them, but you should use them even if your codes don't specify them.

BLOCKING THE JOISTS

1 MARK JOIST CENTERS.

Blocking adds lateral stability to a deck frame and provides additional nailing surfaces for some decking patterns. Mark the midpoint of the deck (half the distance from the house to the beam) on both rim joists and snap a chalk line between the marks across the top of the joists.

2 MARK THE BLOCKING.

Tack a 1×4 on top of each joist near the chalk line to space the joists as your plan specifies. If necessary, pull the joists into proper spacing before tacking the board on. Mark the location of the blocking, offsetting the marks as shown.

Offset blocking makes fastening easier

3 FASTEN THE BLOCKING.

Measure each bay (the space between the joists) and cut 2× blocking to fit. Don't cut all the blocks the same size—the thickness of the joists may vary. Install the blocking with nails or screws on alternate sides of your chalk line. Then fasten the joists to the beam with seismic ties.

INSTALLING DECKING

ecking is the centerpiece of your deck, so choose it carefully. It gets the most use, takes the most abuse, and is one of the deck's most visible elements.

Building centers generally carry several types and grades of decking material. Pressure-treated (PT) wood is a popular choice, of course, but you can use PT lumber just for the framing, and dress up the more visible parts of your deck with fancier stock. See pages 130–132 for more information about selecting lumber.

YOU'LL NEED

TIME: Five to eight hours for a 12×16-foot deck, longer for complex patterns

SKILLS: Measuring, cutting, fastening,

TOOLS: Tape measure, circular saw, hammer, screw gun or drill, chalk line, pry bar, layout square, palm sander

1 MARK THE STARTER BOARD.

Measure from the house to the point where the inside edge of the starter board will fall and mark both rim joists at this distance. Snap a chalk line at the marks. Remember that the position of the first board will depend on whether you will overhang the decking or install fascia.

PRETREAT THE FRAME AND DECKING

If your lumber and decking were not pretreated, apply water repellent. Start with the joists, posts, and framing—it's much easier to treat them while they're still exposed than to treat them from underneath the deck later.

The day before you install the decking, spray both sides of the decking and let it dry.

TIPS TO BETTER DECKING

Decking is one of the most visible elements of your deck, so install it with care. Because naturally resistant woods and KDAT (kiln dried after treatment) lumber won't shrink much, they need a uniform ⅛-inch spacing. Make a spacing jig to speed the job (see page 52). PT lumber will shrink after you install it. Fasten PT boards without spacing.

If you install parallel decking, start with the first board at the house or at the outer edge of the deck. Your decking may not come out exactly, because of board and spacing widths and the size of your deck, so you may need to rip the

last few boards to fit. If you want to hide the size adjustment, install the full-sized starter board at the edge of the deck, and finish with the ripped decking next to the house where it will be less visible. For diagonal and other decking patterns that begin in the center, you may need to reduce the width of deck boards as you approach the edge.

To make the pattern more attractive, offset the joints so they do not fall in a straight line. Center the end of the decking on a joist and attach cleats to the joist so you can keep the fastener away from the end of the board.

Chalk line

2 ATTACH THE STARTER BOARD.

Lay out the decking boards loosely on the deck. Align the starter board with the chalk line and drive in two screws or nails centered on each joist. If you have joints, offset them randomly and fasten cleats to the sides of the joists for additional support.

Installing decking *(continued)*

③ SPACE THE BOARDS.

Set a spacing jig (below) against the starter board and pull the next decking board against it. Fasten the second board to the joists, moving the spacing jig along its length as you go. Make sure the decking joists are centered on the joists and strengthened with 2×4 cleats fastened to both sides of the joist under the joint. Predrill the decking (especially near the ends) to minimize splits. Angle the screws slightly toward the joist to strengthen the connection.

④ CHECK THE SPACING.

The width of a decking board may vary along its length. One odd board won't make a difference, but several could throw the boards off parallel over the span of a deck. Measure the distance from the house to the board every third row. Adjust the spacing to keep the decking parallel. Snap a chalk line for reference.

MAKE A SPACING JIG

To space decking evenly, make a spacing jig from a 1×4 and 10d nails spaced the same as the joist spacing (16 inches, for example). Drive them about an inch through the 1×4. Blunt the tips of the nails so they're less likely to mar or snag on the decking.

STAGGER THE JOINTS

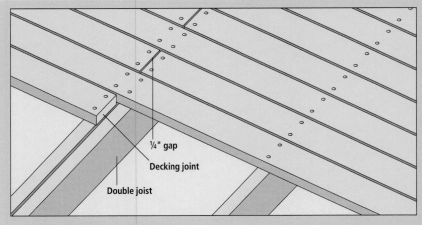

¼" gap

Decking joint

Double joist

Long boards can span a small deck without joints. However, a long deck (certainly one more than 20 feet long) will have joints. Plan ahead so you can install a double joist (or two) in the framing for the joints. When you fasten the decking, alternately offset the joints as shown above. A small gap between the ends of the boards will improve drainage through the decking and the double joist.

5 STRAIGHTEN BOWED BOARDS.

To straighten a bowed board, first start one fastener in the board. Then drive the blade of a pry bar solidly into the joist and force the decking into place. Hold the board in place with one hand and drive the fastener with the other. Then set the second fastener.

To push a bowed edge away from an adjacent board, start the fastener and insert a prybar between the boards. Protect the edge you're prying against with a wide putty knife. Force the board into position and hold it. Then drive the fasteners.

WHICH SIDE UP?

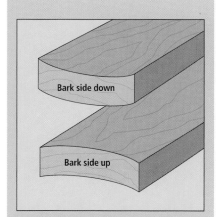

Bark side down

Bark side up

Traditional advice is to install decking with the bark side up so water will drain more quickly. It's been debated for about 30 years. Some studies show that decking installed with the bark side down is less likely to develop splits. Other research says it doesn't make any difference. A practical compromise is to put the best side up and apply a yearly coat of water repellent.

STRAIGHTENING THE STUBBORN ONES

Sometimes even a pry bar won't straighten a bowed board. The best way to prevent this, of course, is to leave these boards at the lumberyard. But if one of them has slipped by you, don't throw it away. You can probably straighten it with a bar clamp, a long clamp designed to hold together wide glue-ups for tabletops and the like. Set the end hook against a prybar inserted in a space between the decking. Position the clamp screw against the bowed board. Turn the screw to force the board in place, then fasten it.

Installing decking *(continued)*

6 ADJUST SPACING IN THE HOME STRETCH.

When you get within three boards of the last one, lay them loosely with ⅛-inch spaces. If the last board fits, fasten all three. If not, lay two and trim the last one, or rip the excess width evenly from all three.

7 FASTEN THE LAST BOARD.

Cut the last board to length, including any overhang. You can trim it with a handsaw after it's in place, but cutting it first is easier. Set the board with the proper overhang on both ends, then fasten it.

8 TRIM THE OVERHANG.

Mark the overhang on the face of both the starter board and the last board. Snap a chalk line between the marks. Tack a 2×4 to the deck to guide your saw blade along the line to trim the wild ends of the decking.

9 BEVEL AND SEAL THE EDGES.

Produce a professional-looking edge by beveling it with a palm sander, a router with a chamfer bit, or a sanding block and 80-grit paper. Seal the cut edge of the decking before installing the railing.

NOTCH DECKING FOR POSTS

1 OUTLINE THE NOTCH.

Set the decking board against the post, then mark the edges of the notch on the decking, adding ⅛ inch. Measure and mark the depth of the notch, then lay out the sides with a layout square.

2× cleat provides nailing surface

2 CUT AND FASTEN.

Cut the notch with a jigsaw and test-fit the cut. Fasten 2× cleats on the posts (on both sides of the notch) to provide a nailing surface. Fasten the board to the joist and the cleats.

Almost all building codes have strict standards for stairs. Exterior tread dimensions are often afforded a little latitude, but codes are quite strict about stringers, materials, and overall construction.

Before you start designing your stairway, review stair-building terminology—it can seem confusing at first. *Total rise* is the vertical distance from the bottom of the stairs to the top of the deck (see page 57). *Unit rise* is the height of one step. *Total run* is the horizontal distance the stairway travels. *Unit run* is the horizontal depth of one tread from front to back.

After code compliance, the most important requirement for outdoor stairs is to make a gradual ascent—short risers and deep treads enhance the safety and comfort of the stairs.

A 3-foot width is the standard minimum, but you may find that a 4- to 6-foot width is more comfortable without adding much to your costs. Use three stringers on stairs 3 feet and wider, and add a stringer for every 2 feet of width.

YOU'LL NEED

TIME: Two to three days to lay out and pour the concrete pad, five to seven hours within that time to lay out, cut, and attach stringers to the deck and treads to the stringers

SKILLS: Working with concrete, measuring, leveling, accurate cutting and fastening

TOOLS: Hammer, straightedge, tape measure, pencil, framing square, level, circular saw, jigsaw or handsaw, sander

ACCESS AND DESIGN.

Stairs serve many purposes in deck designs. They provide access to and from the deck—both to the surrounding landscape and to other levels of the deck. They can greatly increase the seating area of your deck and can be an important element in its style. Stairs come in many forms, from simple, straight-line structures to elaborate multilevel additions with landings. You can install them with or without a landing, but a concrete pad will provide a solid base and a guaranteed long life.

MEASURE THE RISE AND RUN.

Measure the rise and run both to establish the landing location and the cuts on the stringers. On a level yard, measure the rise down from the deck to the ground and the run from that point to the pad. If the yard slopes (and most do), set a level and long board on the deck and measure down to the soil at the location of the pad. Then calculate the individual rise and run (page 57), and adjust the location of the pad to make the steps more comfortable.

Building stairs *(continued)*

Building a landing

1 LAYOUT AND EXCAVATE.

A concrete pad 3 to 4 inches thick should rest on 2 inches of gravel and should have reinforcing wire mesh. Lay out the site with a 4×8 sheet of plywood or batterboards and lines (page 36). Excavate 6 inches deep.

2 BUILD THE FORMS.

Use 2×6 lumber to build forms, cutting and staking each piece as you go. Drive the stakes flush or below the tops of the forms so they won't interfere with the screed when you level the concrete (Step 5). Square the corners with a framing square.

3 LEVEL THE FORMS.

Level the forms and make sure their edges are flush at the corners. Then shovel in crushed gravel and tamp it. You won't need a power tamper for this small site; make a plywood tamper with 2×4 handles. Tamp the gravel to 2 inches deep.

4 BACKFILL, REINFORCE.

Backfill the forms to stabilize them. Lay in a section of wire reinforcing mesh. Set the wire on dobies (from your home center) to keep it at the right height, or pull it up with a rake when you pour the concrete.

5 SCREED THE SURFACE.

Mix the concrete in a wheelbarrow (page 40) and shovel it into the excavation. Then screed the surface (level it) by pulling a long 2×4 across it, see-sawing the board. Screed again if necessary and fill in low spots.

6 SLIP-PROOF THE PAD.

Smooth the surface with a wood or metal float, working in wide arcs and keeping the leading edge of the float raised slightly. When the concrete has started to set up (it resists pushing with your thumb), drag a broom across it to make a nonslip surface.

7 SEPARATE THE FORMS.

Concrete will stick to wood forms like glue, sometimes even if you coat the forms with motor oil. To get them to pop off more easily, slide a pointed trowel between the forms to a depth of about 2 inches.

8 EDGE THE PAD.

A round edge on the pad will help prevent chipping. Insert an edger inside the forms and work it back and forth with its leading edge raised slightly. When the concrete has set up, remove the forms and let it cure for a week. Then cut stringers.

CHOOSE THE RIGHT LUMBER FOR STRINGERS

Stringers carry the weight of the stairs. Choose straight, clear 2×12s with maximum vertical grain. Clear lumber (without knots) is expensive, but it enhances the safety of the stairs.

STEP COMFORTABLY

For safe, comfortable stairs, apply this simple formula: Twice the unit rise (the height of each step to the top of the tread) plus its run (the front-to-back depth of the tread) should equal between 24 and 27 inches.

A standard set of stairs has risers of about 7 inches and runs of 11 inches, for a total of 25 inches.

RISE & RUN: WHERE WILL IT ALL END?

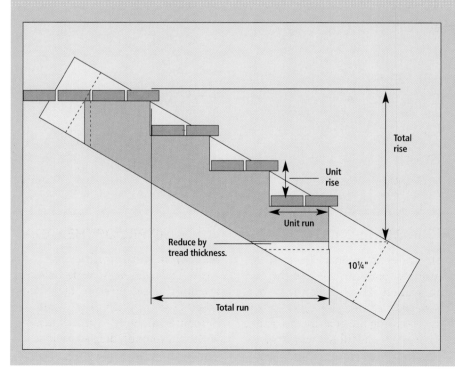

To calculate rise and run, divide the total rise (say 58 inches) by the unit rise you want (7 inches). For this example, the result is 8.2.

Round that to the nearest whole number, 8. This is the number of steps.

Then divide the total rise by the number of steps to find the exact unit rise (58 inches/8=7¼ inches). So each step is 7¼ inches tall.

Now multiply the unit run by the number of steps, minus one (remember, the last step is the deck surface). In this case 11 inches ×7 = 77 inches.

So the stairway will end 77 inches from the deck. That's where you should build the landing.

Building stairs *(continued)*

Constructing the stairs

1 OUTLINE THE STRINGER.

Once you've determined the dimensions of the treads and risers, outline the stringer on a 2×12. Use a framing square with stair gauges, setting the tongue (the short side) of the square at the unit rise and the blade at the unit run.

2 CUT THE OUTLINE.

Cut the top and bottom of the stringer and test its fit between the deck and the landing. Then use a circular saw to cut the outline, stopping the saw blade just short of the intersection of the lines.

3 FINISH THE CUTS.

Finish the cuts with a jigsaw or sharp handsaw, but don't cut deeper than the intersection of the lines. Keep the saw lined up in the circular-saw kerf.

4 OUTLINE THE REMAINING STRINGERS.

Set the cut stringer on the second 2×12 and position it so you can make the same cuts. Clamp the boards together tightly and use the cut stringer as a template to mark the second one. Hold your pencil at a slight angle to make sure it follows the contour of the cuts exactly.

5 ATTACH THE STRINGERS.

Depending on your design, you will either attach the stringers to one of the outer joists or to a crossbrace fastened below one of them. Mark the framing for both outside stringers and snap a chalk line between the marks. This line shows the top of open stringers and the plane of metal cleats on closed stringers. Square the stringers to the deck frame and attach them with angle brackets.

6 ADD THE TOE-KICK.

There are several ways to anchor the bottom of the stringers ("Attachment Options," right). These stringers have been notched for a toe-kick—a 2×4 fastened to the concrete pad. Cut the toe-kick and predrill holes for lag screws, then position the toe-kick.

Using the predrilled holes, mark the pad with a small masonry bit. Remove the toe-kick and drill the pad with a masonry bit to fit the lag-screw shields. Attach the toe-kick to the landing with lag screws, and attach the stringers to the toe-kick.

ATTACHMENT OPTIONS

Gravel base

2×4 (anchor with landscape spike)

Angle bracket

Masonry anchor

Concrete base

Lag screws

Attach stringers to footing. On a gravel pad, attach two 36-inch 2×4s to the bottoms of the stringers and drive landscape spikes through them into the gravel. On a concrete pad, space the outside stringers 36 inches apart, center the middle stringer, and attach with masonry anchors.

7 FASTEN THE TREADS.

If your outside stringers are open, cut the treads with a 1½-inch overhang on both sides. If the stringers are closed (page 60), cut the treads to fit between them. Predrill holes for the fasteners—three per joint for a 2×12 or 2×10 tread, two for narrower boards. Fasten the treads to the outside stringers with nails or screws, then from underneath, fasten the tread to the stair brackets.

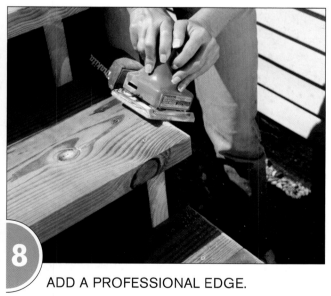

8 ADD A PROFESSIONAL EDGE.

Once the treads are in place, chamfer the edges to improve their appearance. You can use a palm sander or a sanding block and 80-grit paper. A block plane would also work. Whatever the method, keep the angle as consistent as possible.

Building stairs *(continued)*

Making closed stringers

1 OUTLINE THE TREADS.

Using a framing square and the same techniques for marking an open stringer (previous page), outline the tread locations on the stringer stock. Make the top and bottom cuts and test-fit the stringer between the deck and ground. You'll be able to position the stair cleats much easier (Step 2) if you outline the thickness of the tread and mark the location of the cleat.

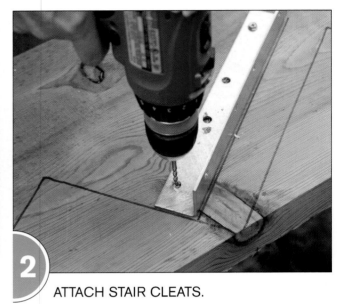

2 ATTACH STAIR CLEATS.

You can fasten stair cleats to the closed stringers either before or after attaching the stringers to the deck. If you're doing it before, set the 2×12 on a work surface with the cleats and fasteners within reach. Position one end of the cleat on the line and predrill one fastener hole. Drive the fastener at this end, line up the cleat, and predrill and drive the remaining fasteners. Install the remaining cleats.

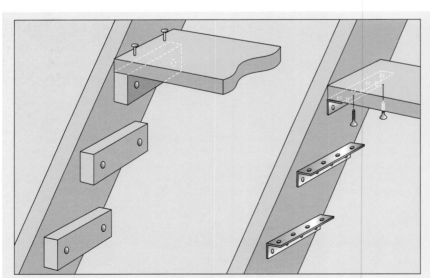

A SOLID STRINGER ALTERNATIVE.

Depending on the width of the stairs, closed stringers may be used alone or with notched stringers in the middle of wider stairs. After you attach the stringers to the deck, you can fasten the treads either to wooden cleats or metal stair brackets. Brackets are fastened from underneath, which is more difficult, but leaves them invisible. Don't rely on screws driven from the outside of the stringer into the ends of the treads.

3 ATTACH THE STRINGERS.

Mark the framing for the top of the stringers and snap a chalk line. Attach the stringers to the framing with angle brackets, then square them. Fasten the stringers to the landing and the cleats to the stringers if you haven't done so already.

4 ATTACH THE TREADS.

Fasten the treads to the cleats with the fastener of your choice (or the one required by local codes). Depending on the height of the stairs and the amount of room underneath, this can be difficult. Always work from the top down to make it easier to reach under the treads. Fasten the ends of the treads first, then the middle brackets.

NOTCHING A POST

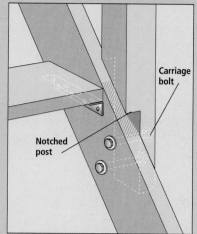

Carriage bolt

Notched post

If posts support both the stringer and a stair railing, consider notching the posts to improve the looks of your stairs. Set the post in place, plumb it, then mark the intersection of the stringer and post. Cut the notch and fasten with carriage bolts.

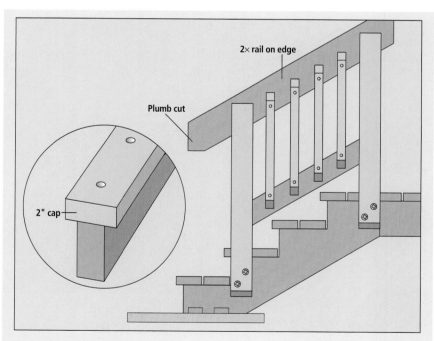

2× rail on edge

Plumb cut

2" cap

ADD A STAIR RAIL.

Match the stair railing with the deck railing style. Use similar balusters spaced at the same interval.

Handrails must be easy to grasp. Adding a 2× cap rail will make the stairway more safe.

Prepare and fasten posts and balusters the same way as for the deck railing (pages 62–65). Make plumb cuts on the top rail.

⚠ CAUTION

FOR COMFORT AND SAFETY, ADD HANDRAILS

Municipal codes generally require a railing on stairs containing three or more risers. But all stairs can be made safer by adding a railing. Everyone understands the added security of having a solid object to grasp when moving from one step to the next. Railings are important if your deck is going to be used by the very young or old. Think safety even if your deck has a one-step level change. Avoid stumbles by adding a strip of yellow reflective tape to steps for greater visibility.

Railings do more than add a safety feature to your deck. They establish the style and the limits of the space. Your local building codes will define standards of a safe deck railing (see right). But those standards probably won't affect your nearly endless number of design choices and construction techniques.

The most common railings are similar to a traditional picket fence. A typical framework consists of 4×4 posts bolted to the outer joists, spanned by 2×4 rails and a 2×6 cap rail, with the balusters providing the infill and much of the style.

The photos on these pages show a simple, attractive design, and like most railings, the rails are attached first, then balusters, then the cap rail.

When installing the posts, the deck overhang can get in the way, but you can either notch the post or notch the decking so the bottom of the post rests flat against the joist. Notching the decking reduces the possibility of weakening the posts.

To prevent sagging railings, keep the spans between posts at 6 feet or less, and use rails-on-edge designs. Bolt each post to the frame with two ⁷⁄₁₆-inch bolts. Creating level lines is especially important because railings are seen against the background of the house. Use a water level—not a line level or level-and-long-board—to place railing elements.

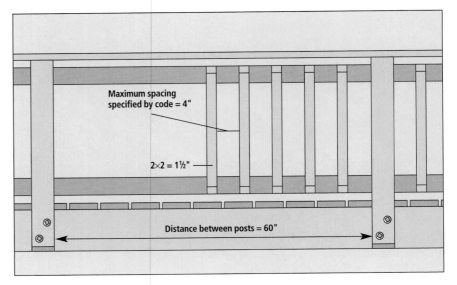

YOU'LL NEED

TIME: About 16 hours to build railings for a 12×16-foot deck

SKILLS: Measuring, cutting, fastening, leveling

TOOLS: Circular saw, mitersaw, post level, 4-foot level, 2-foot level, drill, spade bits, twist drill, socket wrench, spacing jig, hammer, water level, chisel

CALCULATE BALUSTER SPACING.

Building codes specify the maximum baluster spacing. Here's how to calculate uniform baluster spacing.

Add the width of one baluster (here, 1½ inches) and the maximum spacing (4 inches). Divide this total (5½ inches) into the space between posts to find the number of balusters: 60 inches/5½ inches =10.9. Round up to 11 balusters.

Then calculate the actual spacing. Multiply the number of balusters by the width: 11×1½ inches=16½ inches. Subtract that from the post spacing: 60 inches-16½ inches=43½ inches. Divide this by the number of spaces, which is always one more than the number of balusters, to determine the final spacing between balusters: 43½ inches/12=3.625 or 3⅝ inches.

1 GANG-CUT THE POSTS.

Cut your posts to a height equal to the height of the railing plus the thickness of the decking and width of the outer joists—less the thickness of the cap rail. Build a jig so you can cut all posts to the same length. Angle the bottom of the posts as an accent.

2 MARK THE BOLT HOLES.

Mark the location of the bolt holes—about 1 inch in from the sides of the post and 1½ inches from the top and bottom of the joist. Stagger the holes to reduce splits. A template will keep the holes consistent. Then drill holes the same diameter as the bolts.

In the image: Maximum spacing specified by code = 4"; 2×2 = 1½"; Distance between posts = 60"

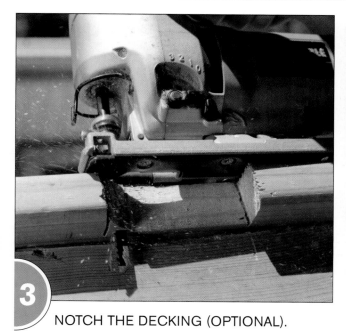

③ NOTCH THE DECKING (OPTIONAL).

Measure each post before you mark the notch on the decking—the width of pressure-treated stock is often inconsistent. Mark the sides of the notch ⅛ inch wider than the post so you don't have to force it to fit. Use a jigsaw to notch the decking . Number each notch and its corresponding post on masking tape.

④ INSTALL THE POSTS.

Hold each post in position and have a helper plumb it with a post level. Whether working alone or with a helper, clamp the post to the joist. Using the holes in the post as a guide, drill holes of the same size through the joist. Insert carriage bolts through the holes, and tighten washered nuts with a socket wrench.

⑤ ATTACH THE RAILS.

You can attach rails flat or on edge, with toenailed fasteners, wooden cleats, or metal brackets. Whatever method you use, predrill the holes to prevent splitting.

ANCHORING THE END OF THE RAILING

Instead of fastening a post where the deck meets the house, use a 2×4 end rail. Cut the 2×4 to the height of the railing and fasten it to the siding with 5-inch lag screws and washers. This connection is far sturdier than a post fastened to the joists and will add stability to the entire length of the railing.

Installing railings *(continued)*

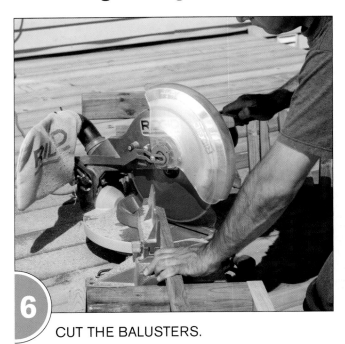

6 CUT THE BALUSTERS.

Cutting the same size balusters will be almost impossible without a cutting jig. Assemble the jig so it supports the end of the baluster and puts the cut end along the fence of your mitersaw. Or clamp the balusters together and cut several of them at the same time on your tablesaw.

7 INSTALL THE BALUSTERS.

When fastening the balusters, use a jig to plumb them and space them uniformly. Check every fourth or fifth baluster with a 2-foot level to make sure it's plumb. Baluster stock is not always a consistent width; you may have to adjust the spacing slightly to make everything come out right.

JOINTS IN THE TOP RAIL

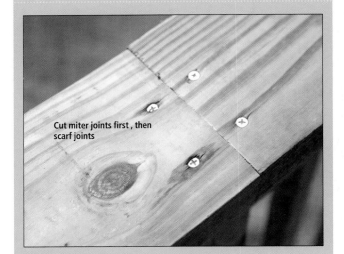

Cut miter joints first , then scarf joints

If your cap rail won't span the entire length of your railing, you'll need to cut joints for it. First, cut the mitered corner and make sure it fits tightly. Then measure from the corner to the center of a post and cut a scarf joint there with a mitersaw. Drive two fasteners on both sides of the joint.

PRODUCTION NOTCHING

Use the same techniques for gang-cutting other railing members when you notch posts. Gang them (clamp them together with their faces flush) and use a T-square when you outline the dimensions of the notch. Cut what you can with a circular saw (use a guide, if possible) then chisel out the rest (opposite).

NOTCHING A POST

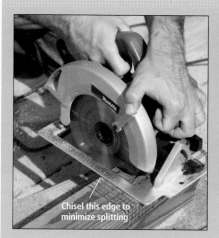

Chisel this edge to minimize splitting

Whether gang-cutting a number of posts or notching a single post, cut kerfs in the notched side with a circular saw. The closer the cuts, the more precise your notch will be.

Remove the waste wood from the notch with a hammer and clean out the face of the notch with a sharp 1-inch wood chisel. Do not sand the surface; sanding will result in rolled edges.

CUTTING PERFECT MITERS

Make your miters match. One reason a miter shows a gap is that the corner is not square. You can't square the corner, but you can modify the miter. Cut both sides of the joint and tack the cap rail in place. Cut through the joint with a circular saw, remove the pieces, and refasten them tightly.

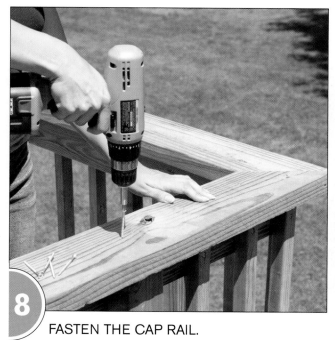

8 FASTEN THE CAP RAIL.

Cap rails are usually cut from 2×6 stock. Cut the rail to length and miter-cut one end. If the board is not long enough to span a railing section, cut a scarf joint in the other end (so it will be centered on a post). Fit the cap rail on top of the railing with an even overhang on each side. Attach the cap rail with two 2½-inch screws into each post and one into the top rail every 2 feet between posts.

9 SNUG THE CORNERS.

Miter joints add style to the corners of a deck, but they are difficult to cut straight and they often separate after about a year. Cut the miter as shown below and drive #8 screws to draw the sides of the joint together. Then drive fasteners down into the posts.

Customizing
YOUR DECK

You'll have pride of accomplishment from building a basic deck, and you'll enjoy the completed project for years to come. Even an uncomplicated rectangle can be a pleasant and useful addition to your landscape. Amenities shown in this chapter, however, can take your deck further. You might view these projects as additions to a basic deck, but with careful planning they will become an integral part of your deck design. If you intend to enhance the style, usefulness, and comfort of your deck or increase privacy and provide protection from the elements, then complex decking and railing patterns, planters, seating, overheads, and privacy screens are necessities. Some of these structures will increase your deck-building costs. Complex decking patterns require more framing and decking. Alternate railing designs can add unusual materials and still more costs. But planters, seating, privacy screens—even a simple arbor—won't break the bank. Whatever the cost, you can consider it a worthwhile investment.

FROM UNUSED PLATFORM TO PAVILION

A simple detached platform lacking ornamentation or amenities may not be very inviting. With a little planning and not a lot of money, you can create an open-air pavilion you'll enjoy frequently. Lattice, textured plywood siding, skylights, trimmed posts, and paint are readily available and inexpensive. All it takes to transform an unused spot into the center of attention is imagination and a careful assessment of needs.

HANDS-ON

There's a lot you can do yourself to add comfort to your deck. All of the projects in this chapter are within the capability of the average do-it-yourself homeowner. Assembling a lattice screen, for example, is a project you can complete in a single weekend.

EVERYWHERE YOU LOOK

A unified deck style creates a strong identity. To keep unity of style from becoming dull uniformity, explore variations on themes. Instead of solid-block seat legs, lighten the look with open 2× supports. Look for ways to alternate the direction of linear elements in the design. Everything doesn't have to be horizontal. Add interest with angles. Mix up geometric elements in a single material and hide that black hole beneath the deck with inexpensive paneling.

Parallel decking is easy to install and cost effective. You can enhance its appearance by laying mixed-length boards and staggering the joints. Parallel decking is mostly a practical choice. For a more intriguing look, cover your deck with one of the patterns at right.

The primary concern with any decking pattern is that the framing supports it adequately.

Herringbone, chevron, and basket weave patterns require wider joists for fasteners at the ends of the boards. To install these patterns, space joints symmetrically on the deck. At each joint, double the joist or triple its width with a 2×4 cleat on both sides. Install full-length pieces first, then the shorter pieces.

Framing for a modular pattern is similar to standard framing except that some joists are doubled or cleated and blocking is installed between some joists to provide nailing surfaces for the alternating deck boards.

Boards are different lengths with most diagonal patterns. This will create extra work and waste.

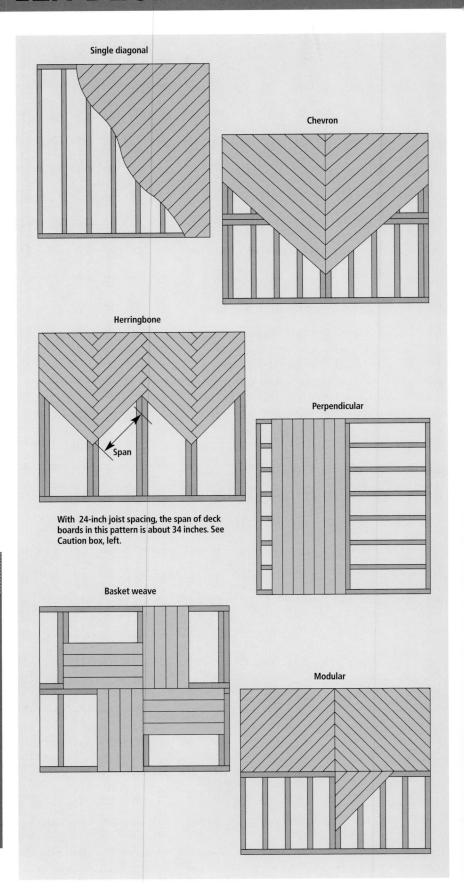

With 24-inch joist spacing, the span of deck boards in this pattern is about 34 inches. See Caution box, left.

CAUTION

CHECK DIAGONALS FOR ALLOWABLE SPANS

In a herringbone or other pattern with diagonal boards, the span is the diagonal distance between joists, not the perpendicular distance. The distance may exceed allowable span lengths. If you have doubts about your decking plan, have a professional designer check it before you begin construction.

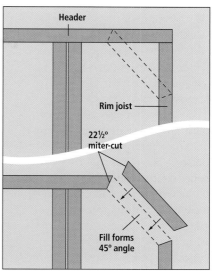

ADD A CENTER STRIP TO CHEVRONS.

A chevron pattern, or any pattern that requires diagonal cuts to meet at a center point, can be difficult to lay precisely. You can make discrepancies in the cuts less apparent by installing a center decking board as shown above. This pattern requires a double row of blocking to provide a nailing surface for both the center board and the miters. Cut both ends of the boards that go between the house and the strip. On the boards that extend to the edge of the deck, cut the angles and leave the ends wild.

ANGLE A CORNER.

If the style suits your house, add a 45-degree corner to a deck with overhanging joists. First, build the frame square, then measure from the corner an equal amount on the rim joist and header. Cut the joist and header at a 22½-degree angle, then mark and cut the corner piece.

TIPS FOR DIAGONALS.

Diagonal decking requires precise 45-degree miters. Practice on scrap before laying your decking. Tack a ¼-inch plywood strip onto the house as a temporary spacer. On the first two boards, miter one end only and set them on the framing with the miters against the spacer. Measure and mark equal distances from the corner frame to the edges of the boards (this assures the boards are diagonal). Fasten the first, then the second board to the decking with a few screws. Install the remaining boards the same way, then snap chalklines at the joists so you can keep the fasteners in line over the surface of the deck. Trim the wild ends of the boards, and remove the spacer.

ATTACHING A SMALL CORNER.

When you're within three feet of a diagonal corner, measure the remaining space to see how wide the last piece will be. Increase the spacing between the last boards so you end up with at least a 5-inch piece. If that doesn't work out, drill pilot holes and fasten the last piece to the adjoining board without spacing.

INSTALLING INVISIBLE DECK FASTENERS

Nail dents, protruding screws or nails, split decking ends, or water puddles in fastener holes will not be problems if you use hidden deck fasteners. Plus, the fastener-free surface looks neater.

These fasteners are more expensive than screws or nails and installation also requires substantially more time and labor. And some fasteners, like track rails, are not practical for low decks. The tracks attach to the sides of the joists, then you need to be able to fasten deck boards from below.

Joist clips (available in several styles) are the easiest to install. You can work from above, and they hold the boards in place with points that dig into the edges of the boards. They space the boards automatically as you lay them. Recessed clips, made for hardwood like Ipe, adapt to any decking. For these, you must form recesses in the edges of the boards with a biscuit joiner.

YOU'LL NEED

TIME: About eight hours to install clips on a 12×16-foot deck, more for a track system

SKILLS: Measuring, cutting, driving fasteners

TOOLS: Tape measure, layout square, mitersaw, cordless drill, pry bar, hammer

Decking clips

1 FASTEN THE CLIPS.

Fasten the first board as specified by the clip manufacturer. Then either attach clips to the joists or to the edge of the second board, depending on the clip style. Use the fasteners that come with the clips; others may not fit.

2 SEAT THE DECKING.

Set the second board in place and with a scrap 2×4 on the joist directly behind the clip, seat the second board about halfway on the clip. Start at one end and work your way down gradually. Install the remaining boards the same way.

Track systems

1 SET THE TRACK ON JOISTS.

Cut sections of track to length, if necessary (some come precut), and line them flush with the top of the joists. Fasten one end, level the track, then fasten the other end. Use only as many fasteners as recommended by the manufacturer.

2 ATTACH THE DECKING.

With a helper positioning the decking above, work from beneath the deck to drive fasteners through the track into the decking. Make sure the decking is seated firmly on top of the joists.

CUSTOMIZE YOUR RAILINGS

Railings offer countless ways to personalize your deck. Baluster styles, post spacing, materials, and ornaments can make striking changes in the appearance of your railing—and your deck. Even the method used to mount the rails will affect the style of your deck. Mount bottom rails flat or on edge inside the post bays or on edge on the surface of the posts. Mount long rails on edge in notched posts. Or mount top rails inside the bays or continuously on top of the posts. Insert 2×2 blusters, slats and battens, or plexiglass or lattice panels. Even the most common beveled baluster design will look different than others with a 2×6 rail cap, finials, and post caps. Check local codes for railing height and baluster spacing requirements.

> IT'S ALL IN THE DETAILS

When you draw your railing plans, sketch in the posts first. Then decide how you want to fill those spaces. Don't immediately think "balusters." Imagine repeated geometric patterns that complement the deck, then sketch those in, too. Adjust the post spacing if your first design won't fit the infill pattern.

> OPEN UP THE VIEW

Infill panels of plastic glazing or tempered glass will let the landscape spill right onto your deck. Plastic glazing can be installed with 2× rails and stops. Tempered glass is heavy and may require steel or aluminum frames.

< CREATE INTRIGUE

Your railing pattern can be a work of art in its own right. The structure of a complex array may take a little more time to plan and build, but designing the infill in sections will help you understand how you should build it. For offset 2× diagonals like these, fasten the longest piece first. Attach the remaining pieces in the order of their length. Then frame the assembly and fasten it between the posts.

Customize your railings *(continued)*

Post options

FULL POST.

Full posts provide solid support to heavy railing designs. They fit into notched decking and are easier to install than other designs.

NOTCHED POST.

Notched posts give railings a lighter look, but provide slightly less lateral strength than full posts. Increase the strength of the railing with rails set on edge.

NOTCHED CORNER POST.

Notching a corner post saves on lumber costs over a doubled-post corner (see opposite page). It imparts a smooth look that fits well into a contemporary theme.

STRENGTHEN A NOTCHED POST

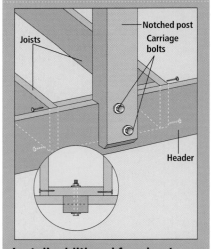

Joists
Notched post
Carriage bolts
Header

Install additional framing to support notched posts. On a header, add 2× blocking between the joists. On rim joists, add blocking between the interior joists to reduce flexing.

Cutting corner notches

Crosscut mark

CUT THE NOTCH.

Outline the notch with a carpenter's pencil so you can see the line when the sawdust flies. For a side post, set the saw to the maximum depth and cut the long lines on each side. Don't cut past the cross-cut mark. For a corner post, set the blade depth to 1½ inches and make the long cuts. Finish the cross cut with a hand saw.

FINISHING A CORNER POST.

Make both the long cuts and a shallow cross cut. Then chisel toward the cross cut with a sharp 1-inch wood chisel to clean out the waste. Continue along the length of the notch in repeated passes until all the waste is removed and the faces of the notch are clean.

Turning corners

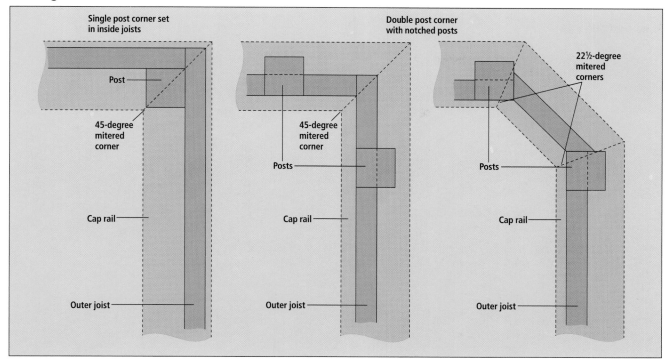

Single post corner set in inside joists

Post

45-degree mitered corner

Cap rail

Outer joist

Double post corner with notched posts

45-degree mitered corner

Posts

Cap rail

Outer joist

22½-degree mitered corners

Posts

Cap rail

Outer joist

You have a choice of designs for the corners of your railings. Setting posts inside corners (hanging the joists on the outside faces of the posts) provides excellent through-post support for overhead structures. You can use this method to support railings on the corners of a cantilevered design.

A two-post corner is the most common design and offers the most lateral strength because side loads, such as people leaning on the railing, are carried by both posts. This construction looks especially good when the spaces between posts are filled with balusters.

Mitered framing lends some distinction to a cantilevered design, and enhances a common rectangle.

Installing through posts

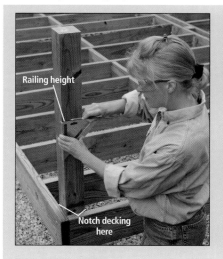

Railing height

Notch decking here

Interior joist

Header

Machine bolts

Blocking

Interior joist

Rim joist

Through posts rest on footings at their bases and continue upward to support railings or overheads. They are most often installed inside the outer joists, so you'll have to notch the decking around them.

This design will put the remaining posts inside the framing. If your post spacing allows it, attach these line posts where an interior joist meets the header. The line posts do not go to the ground.

If a line posts falls in the middle of a rim joist, add perpendicular blocking and fasten it from both sides to keep the post from tilting under stress.

Customize your railings *(continued)*

Railing options

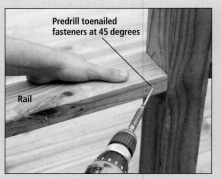

Predrill toenailed
fasteners at 45 degrees

Rail

Cut scarf joints in
surface-mounted
rails and predrill

EXTERNAL RAILS.

Mark the height of the bottom rails on the posts and attach them to the posts with two fasteners, three at the corners. Attach the top rail flush with the top of the posts.

NOTCHED POSTS.

Cut the depth of the notches to exactly 1½ inches and select rail stock with uniform thickness. Fasten the rails with two fasteners, centering joints on the posts.

Making modular infill

2× or 5/4 decking supports and centers balusters on rails.

1 ASSEMBLE THE PARTS.

2 CLAMP THE UNITS.

If the spacing between your posts is uniform (in most cases, it should be) and your design includes internal infill units, you can save a lot of time by assembling all the units at once, then installing them inside the posts.

Set up your construction zone on a clear area of the deck. Tack two decking boards to the deck to support both ends of the balusters, and mark the baluster spacing on both of them. This will keep the balusters centered on the rails. Lay the precut railings edge down and drive one fastener through the rail into the baluster, then fasten the remaining rail. Build the rest of the units, then fasten them to the posts.

Railing units can be installed a lot faster and more exactly if you clamp them in place before driving the fasteners. Support both ends of the bottom rail on scrap to keep the rail level and in place. Clamp the first baluster to the post and drive screws through predrilled, angled holes.

Rail, baluster, and post styles

As long as you meet building-code specifications for spacing and height, what you use to fill in the space between posts is largely up to you. (Some local codes may not allow glass insets and horizontal infill.)

Rails that are installed on edge on either the inside or outside post faces are least likely to sag. Flat rails tend to sag, but you can reduce or even eliminate sagging by centering a 4× support post between the rail and the decking. Fasten flat rails to the posts with rail brackets, toenailed fasteners, wooden cleats, or set them into dadoes cut in the posts.

Railing materials also offer a variety of design options. You can use copper or galvanized steel tubing instead of wood balusters. Copper can be lacquered or coated with a plastic or polymer finish to preserve its color or you can let it age to a blue-green. Steel or aluminum balusters can be inserted as is or painted.

Clear acrylic sheets or glass, where allowed, are ideal for maintaining an open view. Welded hog fencing has even been used to make strong and attractive infill.

Balusters do not have to be vertical. Local codes may prohibit horizontal infill because children can use it as a ladder to climb over the railing. But if kids and codes are not an issue, make simple but stylish infill from horizontal 1×4s or 2×4s. Metal tubing or thick wood dowels offer an attractive alternative.

Whatever you use, remember that wear and gravity will make most horizontal elements sag over time. Make sure they're strong and are solidly supported.

Lattice railing infill provides more privacy than standard railings, yet allows plenty of air to circulate. The lattice can be fixed in place with stops nailed to the posts and to top and bottom flat rails (see page 84).

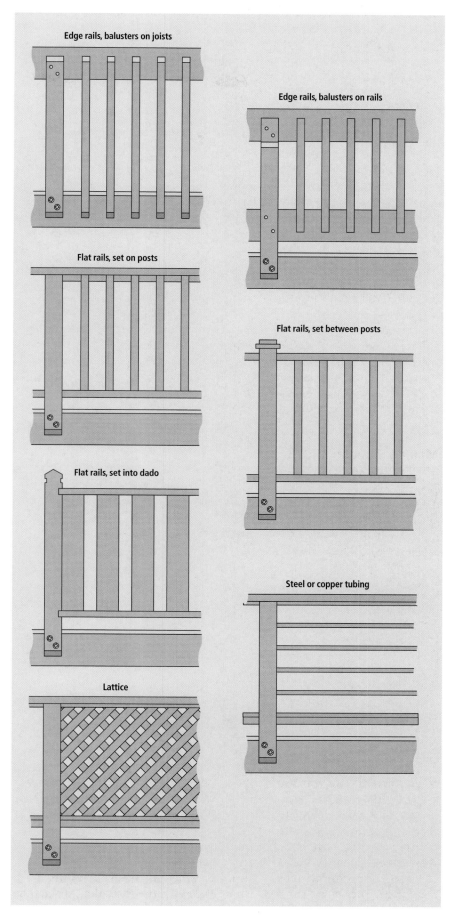

Edge rails, balusters on joists

Edge rails, balusters on rails

Flat rails, set on posts

Flat rails, set between posts

Flat rails, set into dado

Steel or copper tubing

Lattice

BUILDING PLANTERS

Planters overflowing with annuals and perennials can soften the lines of your deck and help link it to your landscape.

Whatever planter you make, be sure that water can drain freely out of the bottom, and plan where that water will go. Drained water trapped in a cavity below the planter can cause decking to rot. Most decorative plants need less than 1 foot of soil depth. Rather than filling a tall planter with more soil than necessary, build a shelf inside it.

Make the planter 18 to 24 inches deep if you will plant shrubs or bushes. Planters for annuals can be smaller. Always build planters with an inch or two of space beneath them to allow for air circulation.

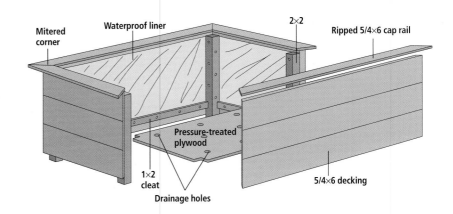

Mitered corner · Waterproof liner · 2×2 · Ripped 5/4×6 cap rail · Pressure-treated plywood · 1×2 cleat · Drainage holes · 5/4×6 decking

BASIC PLANTER CONSTRUCTION.

All planters are basically boxes—four sides and a bottom, perhaps with some kind of optional legs and a cap rail for appearance. Almost any lumber will do; using decking boards for the sides adds to the unity of the deck design. Although you can fasten the corners without corner blocks, using them will create a stronger container for your plantings.

RECYCLE DECK SCRAPS

When you've paid top dollar for good quality lumber, the last thing you should do is add it to the landfill or burn it in the fireplace. Instead, save scraps to build small outdoor projects. (Never burn pressure-treated wood; it releases toxins into the air.)

You'll likely have enough scrap to build a planter or two. Set the planters in corners, along the edge of the deck, or on top of railings. Pressure-treated wood is fine for planters, but redwood and cedar make more attractive accents.

ADD A DECORATIVE TOUCH.

Even simple touches can make a planter more attractive. Once you have the box assembled, draw or scribe lines on the sides, using a layout square to keep them parallel to the edges of the box. Set your circular saw to a depth of about one-third the thickness of the sides and cut grooves along the lines. Use a guide board or rip fence, if necessary. Widen the grooves by making multiple, offset passes with the saw.

Offset planked siding and add a cap

Corner post

Shelf for container

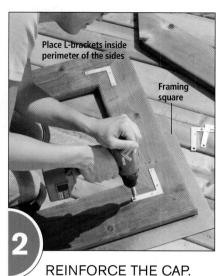

Place L-brackets inside perimeter of the sides

Framing square

1 USE VERTICAL SIDING.

Decking makes good siding for planters. Clamp the pieces together and fasten them to a 2×6 cleat at the bottom. The cleat holds the boards and acts as a stop for the shelf. Fasten the sides at the corners and cut decking for the shelf.

2 REINFORCE THE CAP.

A cap will keep the top of the siding together and improve the appearance of the planter. Cut it from decking and miter the corners. Fasten L-brackets to hold the corners together then use finishing nails to fasten the cap to the sides.

SMALL PLANTS, SMALL PLANTER.

Railings are just as good a spot for planters as any (just don't block your views). Use 1× stock of the same species used elsewhere in your deck (from fascias, for example), and build the box wide enough to fit over the cap rail. These little units are also good for lining the edges of openings in the deck.

2×6 or 2×10 cap, depending on the planter size

Offset 1× siding

Gap for circulation

PUT YOUR PLANTS ON WHEELS

Make your container garden a moveable feast for the eyes by putting put some of your planters on wheels.

Design the planter so the sides extend below the bottom of the corner posts by the height of the wheel (use small swivel casters), minus ¼ inch (so the box won't drag on the deck).

Assemble the planter, turn it upside down and mark the centers of the corner posts. Drill holes in the center for the caster ferrule (what the caster swivels in). Drive the ferrule in and tap in the stem of the caster.

CONSTRUCTING DECK SEATING

Deck seating is more than just a place to sit down. Seating can define the perimeter of your deck and suggest boundaries on the deck for different areas of use.

A well-designed built-in bench can contribute to the style of your deck almost as much as a well-designed railing—it's just shorter.

Benches should be between 15 and 18 inches high with seats at least 15 inches deep. For comfortable lounging, seats can be up to 30 inches deep. Build your benches from the same lumber as your railings so they won't look like an afterthought.

2×10 leg

Machine bolts (third bolt at bottom of leg not visible)

Seat rail

Cleat gives decking a nailing surface

YOU'LL NEED

TIME: From six to eight hours for a 5-foot bench, depending on the design and length

SKILLS: Measuring, cutting, driving fasteners

TOOLS: Tape measure, circular saw, cordless drill, socket wrench, square, screwdriver, hammer, sander, router

CAUTION

DON'T SUBSTITUTE SEATS FOR RAILINGS

Backless built-in perimeter seating is not a substitute for railings. If you build a 15-inch bench on a deck for which codes require a railing, building inspectors will probably insist you add a railing. Children will stand on benches, so railings behind benches need to be higher to provide adequate protection. Build a back on the bench when you need a railing too.

PERPENDICULAR TO JOISTS.

Mark the joists for the 2×10 legs, placing them the same distance from the header. Cut the legs and fasten them with three machine bolts in predrilled holes. Then insert vertical blocking between the joists to keep the bench from rocking side to side. Cut seat rails to match the depth of the bench seat and screw them to the legs. Add cleats to the outside of the leg so the decking cutout will have a nailing surface beneath it.

Cleat gives decking a nailing surface

2×10 leg

PARALLEL TO JOISTS.

Mark the joists to space the 2×10 legs at about half the total width of the seat slats. Machine-bolt the legs to the joists and block the joists to keep the seat from rocking. Cut the seat rails to about 16 inches for a 19-inch bench seat and screw them to the legs. Then cleat both sides of the legs to give the decking a nailer. You can install the seat slats before or after finishing the decking, but if you do the slats first, you may bump your head when you attach the deck.

Perimeter bench

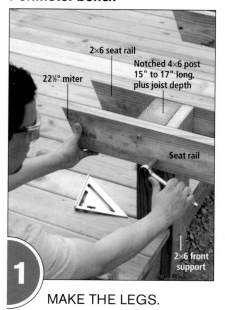

22½° miter
2×6 seat rail
Notched 4×6 post 15" to 17" long, plus joist depth
Seat rail
2×6 front support

1 MAKE THE LEGS.

Cut the front 4×6 post and the 2×6 support 15 to 17 inches long, plus the depth of the joist. Clamp the boards to the outer joists and drill carriage-bolt holes. Fasten the seat rails to the supports with lag screws.

2× seat slats

2 FASTEN THE SLATS.

Cut seat slats to overhang the rails by 1 to 3 inches. Use 2×2 slats, as shown, or 2×3s ripped from wider stock. Set up an overhang jig as shown (below left) and drive one fastener through each end of the slat.

½" plywood spacer
2×6 seat rail
2×2

OVERHANG JIG.

For a 1½-inch overhang, clamp a 2×2 to the seat rails. Line up the ends of slats flush with the jig and screw them to the rails, spacing them with a plywood spacer. Square the slats to the rails and attach the other ends the same way.

Butcher block bench

LAMINATE A BUTCHER BLOCK BENCH.

Cut each piece of the bench to length before assembling the bench. Build it with a full-length slat and short leg on the outside and a short slat and full-height leg next, as shown. Align each slat carefully, flush at the top, then mark their positions and laminate them with screws and glue. Stagger the screws to avoid splitting the wood. Finish the bench to match the deck.

Built-in deck perimeter seating must be designed to carry a heavy load, and nothing can provide better support than the railing posts. A perimeter bench is easy to build, and because the railing posts support it, it doesn't require much extra lumber.

If possible, posts should be located no more than 4 feet apart for proper support. Support bench spans wider than that with a 2×4 rail centered on the span and supported by short legs cut from 4×4s. This kind of seating can line the perimeter of the deck.

YOU'LL NEED

TIME: Up to a full day to construct one section

SKILLS: Measuring, cutting, fastening

TOOLS: Circular saw, drill, hammer, sanding block or power sander

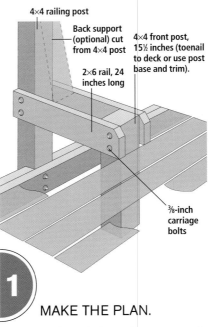

4×4 railing post

Back support (optional) cut from 4×4 post

4×4 front post, 15½ inches (toenail to deck or use post base and trim).

2×6 rail, 24 inches long

⅜-inch carriage bolts

1 MAKE THE PLAN.

Build your bench from the same stock as your railing, using the dimensions shown above. Be sure modifications to this design do not reduce the strength of the bench.

2 BOLT POST.

Cut bench posts to the same dimensions as your railing posts, predrilling them for carriage bolts and either notching the decking or the post, consistent with the railing posts.

3 FASTEN SEAT RAILS.

Using a framing square, mark the location of the front post. Cut the post from 4×4 stock and toenail it to the decking or fasten it with a post base (trim the base later). Clamp the seat rails to both posts, drill them, then fasten them with carriage bolts.

4 FASTEN THE SLATS.

Cut seat slats to length from 2×2, 2×3 or 2×4 stock, allowing at least a 1½-inch overhang. Fasten the slats to the rails with one or two fasteners at each end, depending on the slat width. Space the slats with a spacing jig (page 52).

5 FASTEN THE CAP RAIL.

Cut and install the back slats the same way. Then cut and fasten the 2×6 cap rail, mitering the corners. Sand the surfaces of the cap rail smooth and finish it to match the railing and deck.

Support for an overhead structure on a deck depends on the size of the overhead and its location on the deck. The two corner posts of the deck can support a simple shade structure on one end of a deck. A pergola over a small deck could be supported on the corner posts.

These examples require through posts, which are anchored in footings and extend past the deck to the top of the structure. You can attach through posts to the inside or outside of joists, depending on the design (page 73).

To simplify construction use a single-post corner (page 73) instead of a double-post design. In all other cases, a four-post overhead will have at least two posts supported by the decking and the framing under it.

Use the beam and joist span tables, on page 133 when computing spans. That way, you won't have to worry about the ceiling sagging under its own weight.

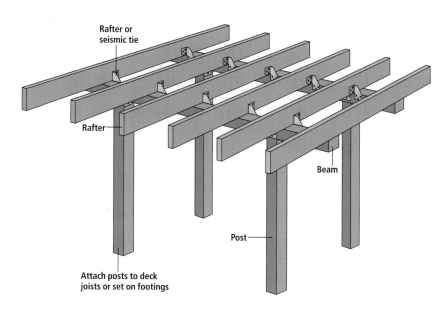

Rafter or seismic tie

Rafter

Beam

Post

Attach posts to deck joists or set on footings

BUILD A FREESTANDING OVERHEAD.

Overheads can be freestanding structures or attached to the house. At a minimum, freestanding overheads need support at their corners—posts set in a solid base (a footing or tied securely to the deck frame). If you're retro-fitting an existing deck with an overhead, you'll have to either take up some of the deck to get at the framing or provide perimeter support with new posts anchored in footings.

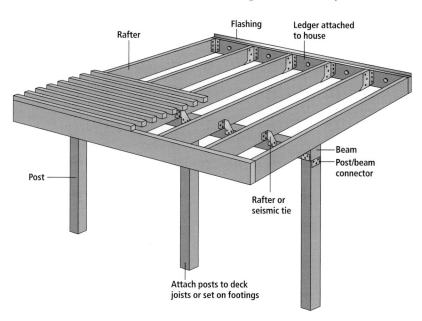

Rafter

Flashing

Ledger attached to house

Post

Beam

Post/beam connector

Rafter or seismic tie

Attach posts to deck joists or set on footings

ATTACH AN OVERHEAD TO THE HOUSE.

Overheads can be supported in part by a ledger attached to the house (see pages 28–33 for ledger installation). Add a beam supported by posts fastened to the deck joists or set on post footings. Attach the rafters to the beam with seismic ties to give it more stability.

SIMPLY FOR LOOKS
An overhead usually provides shade. This one supports vines for shade on one side and lets sunlight onto the deck on the other.

Building overhead structures *(continued)*

AN AIRY ATTRACTION
Some overhead structures are designed primarily for visual appeal. Here cased 6×6 posts with a double cornice trim support arched beams. What could easily have become a massive design is lightened with the 2× slat ceiling spaced to let the light play both on the structure and the deck below.

BEAUTIFUL ENDINGS
A few graceful lines cut into the ends of rafters and beams creates a sculpted effect. The most appealing overhead designs are built in layers, each composed of smaller pieces spaced increasingly closer. The crisscrossed framing adds stability, enhances the profile, and makes a natural trellis for climbing vines.

ELEGANT DETAILS
Here's a good way to combine the massive with the delicate to create harmony. Framed lattice becomes a fretwork along the upper perimeter, an effect enhanced by its off-white coat of paint. Rough weathered beams make a surprising yet elegant contrast with the chippendale railing panels.

AN OUTDOOR ROOM
This overhead adds only a moderate amount of shade. Its primary function is to define the ceiling for this stylish outdoor room. This deck is an extension of the house, and all of its elements combine to make the room inviting.

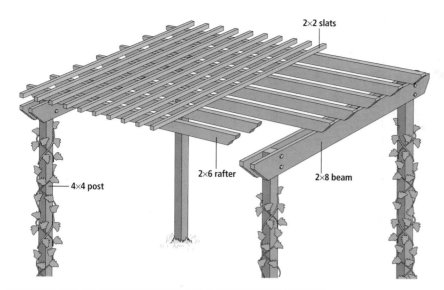

2×2 slats

2×6 rafter

2×8 beam

4×4 post

BRACING POSTS

It's not easy to tell when to brace posts supporting an overhead structure. Local codes may not offer definitive answers. If your overhead is lightweight (loosely spaced slats, for example) and if one side is connected to a ledger at the house, you probably won't need bracing. On the other hand, for a top-heavy overhead on a freestanding deck, assume that you should brace the posts. For everything in between, build without bracing and check the stability of the structure before deciding. For guidance on bracing, see page 111.

VARY THIS BASIC DESIGN TO SUIT YOUR DECK.

This overhead is simple to build and can be adjusted easily to provide the degree of shading you want. Double 2×8 beams span posts but could extend from a ledger. The 2×6 rafters set 16 inches on center can safely traverse spans up to 12 feet. Use rafter ties or 10d nails (through both sides) to fasten rafters to beams. Note that beam and rafter ends have matching tapers. (You can also use any of the other decorative cuts shown below.) Attach a top layer of 2×2 slats, spaced 4 to 8 inches apart; drive 8d nails through the slats into the rafters, or use lattice for the top.

BRACING POSTS ON THE DECK SURFACE

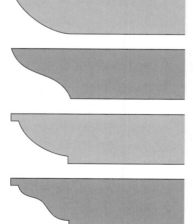

Overhead posts centered between the joists need bracing. Cut a 4×4 to fit between the joists and lag screw it in place, flush with the top of the joists. Then screw 2×4 cleats to the joists on both sides of the 4×4. After you've laid the decking, drill through the deck and 4×4 brace, insert a bolt, and fasten the post anchor.

CHOOSE A DECORATIVE RAFTER CUT.

One of the keys to making an attractive overhead is cutting dressed-up rafter ends. Find a decorative detail on the house or in the yard, then transfer it to the rafter ends. Make a template of plywood, hardboard, or cardboard, trace the design on each rafter, then cut.

FRAMING A LATTICE SCREEN

Lattice is popular screening material, suitable both for overheads and privacy screens. Usually sold in 4×8-, 2×8-, and 4×6-foot sheets, it's decorative and easy to install. Standard panels are ½ inch thick; but use ¾-inch lattice—it's tougher and will last longer, with almost no maintenance. The size of the spacing also varies.

Lattice is easily framed between 1× stops attached to posts and rails. For a more finished appearance, trim the panels with milled moldings (below).

Plastic lattice panels look similar to painted wood and are worth considering if low maintenance is your chief concern.

YOU'LL NEED

TIME: About one hour per sheet after the frame is built

SKILLS: Measuring, cutting lattice and trim

TOOLS: Handsaw or circular saw, hammer, screwdriver or cordless drill, square, tape measure

1 MAKE THE FRAME.

Plumb and fasten the posts to the rim joists or header (page 72) and attach rails. Mark the top and bottom of the posts inside the bays ¾ inch from the edge and snap a chalkline between the marks. Mark the inside edges of rails the same way. Finish-nail 1× stops at this line.

2 FASTEN THE LATTICE.

Brush sealer on the edges of the lattice and paint or stain the panels before you hang them. Cut the panels to fit the bays and set them against the nailers. Hold the lattice in place and install 1× stops with finish nails. Do not drive fasteners into the lattice—only into the posts and rails.

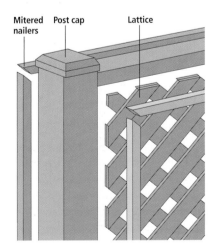

DRESS UP THE FRAME.

Details make a lot of difference in panel construction. Miter the corners of stops and nailers, top the posts with decorative caps, and add a cap rail to the top rail.

Framing options

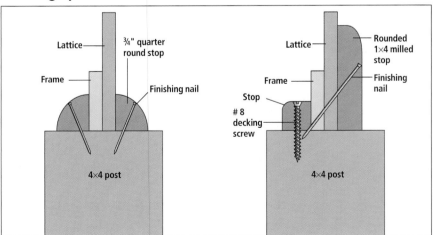

USE MILLED STOCK.

Stops and nailers for lattice can take many forms. If you want to dress up the looks of your lattice frame, attach quarter-round molding or rounded milled stock to the edges. Always make sure you drive the finishing nails into the post and not into the lattice. Seal or finish the milled stock before you install it.

BUILDING PRIVACY SCREENS

Lattice is ideal for screening and for moderate privacy. Some deck sites, however, need more privacy than lattice can provide. The more privacy you need, the more solid the screen needs to be. Board-and-slat infill, louvers, and open panels will close off the view but let some of the breeze flow through. You can build these structures as railing infill or fences if the screen needs to be placed off the deck itself.

YOU'LL NEED

TIME: About three hours per 6-foot bay, after setting posts

SKILLS: Measuring, squaring, plumbing, cutting, and fastening

TOOLS: Handsaw or circular saw, hammer, screwdriver or cordless drill, square, tape measure

SUPPORT THE SCREEN

The screens on this page are adaptations of popular fences. Their functions are similar—almost all fence designs can be built as railing infill. A small screen can be supported by posts bolted to the deck framing. A large screen should be connected to posts anchored to footings, especially if the screen will have to withstand heavy winds. Instead of building a screen onto a deck, consider installing a screen or a fence some distance away from the deck (see page 14).

LOUVERS.

Louvered screens (or fences) offer some of the same benefits as latticed screens, but they adapt to different landscape styles better. Louvers partially block the view and let in cooling breezes. They're also an effective design element in a setting that needs strong vertical lines.

Angled at 45 degrees, 1×6 louvers are too wide for frames built with 4×4s, 2×4s, and 1×4s. You can rip them to fit, install them at a flatter angle, or build framing with nominal 6-inch-wide lumber.

BOARDS AND SLATS.

Board-and-slat infill, in either a fence or a railing, will increase your privacy and will add a little variety to the design of a solid board fence.

This design tends to look better with 1×4 boards and 1×2 slats. Make a spacer to hang on the rails to keep the spacing uniform throughout the panel.

SOLID BOARDS.

A solid board fence offers the most privacy and should be used carefully so you don't feel like you're being walled in. Use this construction for fences away from the deck site. Or place isolated panels at strategic points on the railing to provide almost complete privacy. They will add architectural contrast to other elements in the deck.

Open space under a raised deck can mar the looks of even the most well-designed structure. Short shrubs at the rear of a colorful planting bed will hide the empty space and provide a pleasant transition from the deck to the yard. Lattice frames are another easily installed screen.

In a damp climate, skirting will need to provide enough ventilation to prevent moisture problems. In dry climates, ventilation isn't a primary need. If you make your skirting from 1× lumber instead of lattice, space the boards at ½-inch intervals. Wider spacing can make the pattern more interesting. You can use vinyl lattice if low (or no) maintenance is important to you—it won't rot and needs no painting.

Provide a nailing surface for lattice with nailers inside the posts and along the bottom edge, and fasten framed sections to the nailers. That way, it will not cave in if you bump it with the lawn mower. If you want to use the space under a deck for storage, frame the sections so you can remove and reattach them.

YOU'LL NEED

TIME: Eight to ten hours to install about 40 feet of lattice

SKILLS: Creating a plan, cutting, measuring, fastening

TOOLS: Tape measure, post level, cordless drill, hammer, circular saw, handsaw, framing square and layout square, mason's line

Install a permanent skirt

ATTACH A NAILING SURFACE.

Cut pressure-treated 2×2s or 2×4s to fit between the posts and toenail them at the top and bottom of the opening. Fasten the bottom nailer from 2 to 3 inches above the ground. Recess the nailers from the front edges of the posts if you want a reveal around the edges.

If the open space is 2 feet long or less, you probably won't need vertical supports, but in larger openings, fasten vertical 2×s also. This provides a solid base for the lattice panel. Cut and install all the 2× framing before installing the lattice.

FASTEN THE LATTICE.

Using the same kind of wood as you used in the railings, cut lattice panels to fit the openings and seal, stain, or paint all of the surfaces to protect them from the elements. Then either frame the panels first, driving short screws from the rear of the lattice into 1×4 mitered frames, or screw the lattice panels to the 2× nailers and fasten the trim to the top of it.

Install an accessible skirt

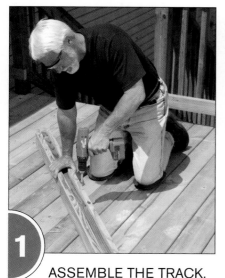

1 ASSEMBLE THE TRACK.

Removable lattice will need both solid support around its edges and a track which will allow you to remove it. Cut a pressure-treated 4×4 bottom rail to fit between the posts and fasten 1× nailers along both of its top edges. This will leave a 2-inch open track in the center of the rail.

2 SET THE BOTTOM RAIL.

Set the 4×4 bottom rail between the posts and attach it to the posts with brackets or toenailed fasteners. If the horizontal span is more than 3 feet, drill the rail and drive timber spikes into the ground at 2-foot intervals.

3 FASTEN THE NAILERS.

In openings 6 feet or longer, cut 2×4 or 4×4 vertical supports and toenail them to the bottom rail and joist in the center of the opening. Cut 2× nailers to fit the top and sides of each space and nail them to the posts, joists, and vertical supports, 2¾ inches back from the front of the posts.

4 INSTALL THE FRAMES.

Cut lattice to fit the openings (less ⅛ inch all around) and pre-finish them. Frame the lattice with 1×4 trim, mitering the corners. Drop the bottom edge of the frame into the track on the bottom rail and attach permanent panels with screws driven into the nailers. For removable panels, install sliding bolt locks in the corners. Slide the locks open and lift the panel out to gain access to the space under the deck.

Install a solid skirt

For solid skirting, use the techniques on this page to cut and fasten nailing surfaces for the boards. Use plywood siding, tongue-and-groove boards, or any other siding of your choice, fastening it to the nailing surfaces.

Deck
VARIATIONS

Before you draw your deck plans, consider some of the alternatives to a basic rectangular shape. If a rectangular deck doesn't seem to fit your yard or your needs, other deck styles probably will. Wraparound decks, for example, can offer substantially more space, and that increases the versatility of your project. So can multilevel and elevated decks. You can even build multiple platform decks, tiered down a gentle slope. Or you can build several decks that overlap on level ground to solve many size and placement problems. These variations can also bring quick solutions to other problems posed by terrain and unusual home architecture. The designs shown on the following pages were built to meet specific needs and situations. But there's no reason you can't borrow aspects of these designs and incorporate them into your deck.

SPA SPACE

Integrating a spa or hot tub into your deck requires additional framing to support the weight of the tub and the water (over 8 pounds per gallon). By elevating the deck frame slightly, you can make the spa appear to be a sunken pool. When planning to include water features of any kind—even those with fish—pick the pond first. Then design your deck around it.

FREESTANDING FREEDOM

Freestanding decks are often overlooked because a deck is usually attached to the back of the house. By making use of large areas in the yard, a freestanding deck provides both a solitary haven and extra space for large gatherings. Walkways can link a freestanding deck to the yard, gardens, other decks, and the house.

SPLIT THE DIFFERENCE

Raised decks can offer a different view of your landscape. Before you finalize your plans, look out from a second-story window. If there's a view from that vantage point that's just not available from a first-floor deck, you might want to raise the deck to take advantage of it. Or, build the deck between the two floors of the house and build stairs to it from both levels.

WRAPPING DECKS AROUND A HOUSE

Turning a corner or two is one of the simplest ways to add area to a deck and still keep spaces well-defined and separate. You can have one area for large gatherings and another that is a private nook. Dual use is the answer when you want access from more than one doorway.

Decks that wrap around a house increase costs only moderately and add few complications to construction. A wraparound is essentially two decks, with two ledgers and a common beam that unites both sections.

A modest wraparound could include a full-sized deck on one side of the house with a small bump-out on an adjacent side, perhaps to be used for storage. More ambitious decks might surround two or three sides of the house on two or more levels. A narrow deck can serve as a walkway. On sloping lots, wraparound decks make moving around the perimeter of the house much easier.

∧

A SECOND-STORY PORCH
This wraparound deck provides plenty of room for family gatherings and private retreats. The style of this deck complements the home.

∨

SWEEPING VERANDA
This rambling deck features a generous walkway and several areas for lounging and dining, making it ideal for large parties.

WHAT TO DO WITH OBSTACLES

This expansive deck demonstrates the best way to deal with obstacles: Work with them, not against them. Extra framing allows the deck to follow the the exterior walls of the home and surround the shade tree that's an important focal point. Wrapping the deck not only around the house, but also around other elements in the yard, creates a stage for a dramatic design. All of the details make an eye-catching continuous sweep—French doors, tall windows, and repeated lattice patterns help blend indoor and outdoor spaces.

GRAND WALKWAY FOR AN ELEVATED VIEW

A sweeping view often calls for a deck of sweeping proportions. This house already had an open feel, with plenty of large windows and sliding glass doors facing several directions. A deck on only one side of the house would have looked inadequate. When friends gather, they can stroll over a spacious area to take in the view from a number of vantage points. Building a large deck raised this high is a major undertaking; seek design help from the pros.

Plans for a wraparound deck should begin with the decking pattern—the way you want the boards to run. That's because different patterns will require different framing—and possibly a different footing layout—to support it. The variations shown here, however, are all based on the same footing plan. Decking that runs parallel to the side of the house on each section and meets at a right angle is visually pleasing and the easiest to build (below right).

Decking that turns a corner is attractive, but more complicated to frame (top, opposite page). Laying mitered decking can be time-consuming as well, but herringbone corners avoid the need for perfect miter cuts.

Continuous decking (bottom, opposite page) creates a unified appearance. The framing is a bit unconventional, with joists running parallel to the house on one side and perpendicular on the other. The construction, however, is no more complex than for a basic deck.

PERPENDICULAR DECKING.

Framing this wraparound is as simple as framing a single deck—you just do it twice. The foundation for each section starts with its own ledger and ends with its own beam supported by posts and footings. The only peculiarity in this design is the extended ledger. Supporting one section of the deck at the house, it meets with a parallel joist at the corner of the house and the pair continues to the outside post.

Beyond that, calculate framing requirements, such as post size and spacing, and beam and joist spans as if each section were a separate deck—which it is. This design is an excellent way to enlarge an existing deck with a wraparound section.

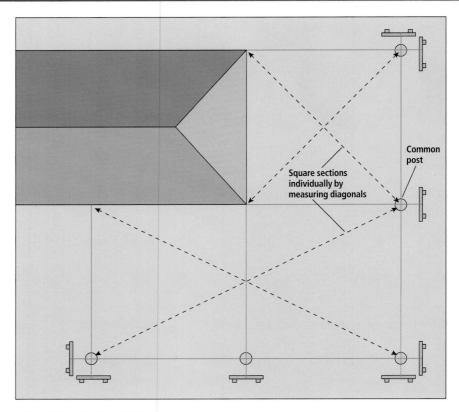

LAY OUT THE DECK.

You can approach the footing layout of almost any wraparound deck by thinking of it as two decks with a common post. Set the position of the common post by running a mason's line from the corner of the house to a batter board. Then treat this post as a line post between the two corners. This way you can square each section with a 3-4-5 triangle or by measuring the diagonals, and center the common post with the others.

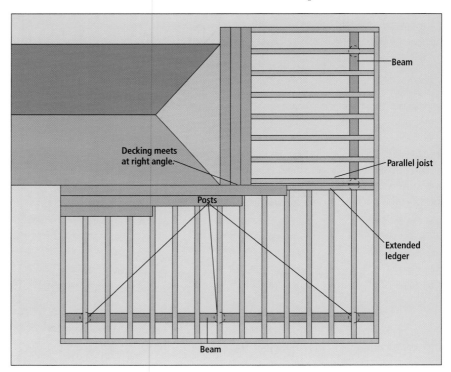

TURNING THE CORNER.

Decking that turns the corner creates a more interesting pattern and looks more professional than other patterns, but it is more difficult to install. You can turn the corner one of three ways—with butted miters, spaced miters, or herringbone joints.

Butted miters are the most difficult to lay. It's not only hard to cut consistent miters, it's doubly difficult to keep the joints perfectly aligned. Even with perfect cuts, decking boards can be slightly off size, and it only takes a couple of those to throw alignment off in a row of joints.

Spaced miters eliminate this problem. Be sure the doubled joist is wide enough to provide a nailing surface for the mitered ends.

A herringbone pattern is the easiest to install and creates a distinctive look. All of these patterns require miter-cut joists and angled joist hangers.

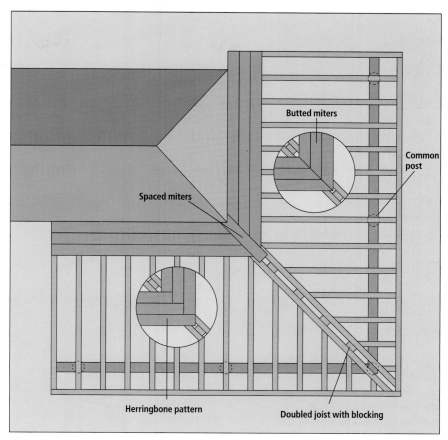

Butted miters

Common post

Spaced miters

Herringbone pattern

Doubled joist with blocking

CONTINUOUS DECKING.

Continuous decking provides an attractive pattern for a wraparound design, but requires different framing and two more footings.

Install ledgers on both sides of the house. Then, on the corner that lines up with the common post, add another footing and post and a beam between the two.

Lap the joists over the common beam and fasten the overlaps together. Plan the decking so the joints don't create an irregular pattern at the corner; usually, it is best to start with a piece that runs only partway along the house, as shown at right.

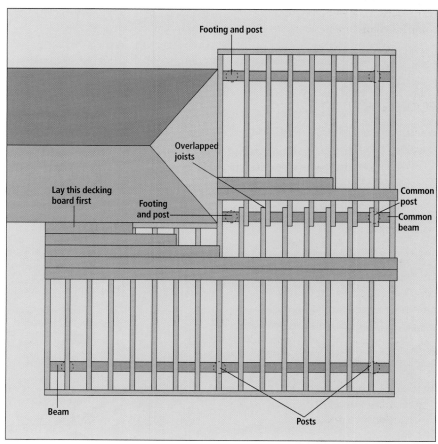

Footing and post

Overlapped joists

Lay this decking board first

Footing and post

Common post

Common beam

Beam

Posts

Multiple decks work well in a number of settings—both as independent structures and as sections stacked and connected with stairs. Independent multiple decks usually have one deck that acts as a balcony and another that serves as the main deck.

A multilevel design is a good solution for slopes. From a tall main deck, smaller connected decks can stairstep down the slope. These smaller sections won't block the view from the main deck and can work as outdoor rooms in their own right, furnished for smaller gatherings. Multilevel decks are effective on two-story houses too. You can use the main-floor deck for entertaining, with a lower section off the walkout basement for a shaded area, and a third level off the upstairs bedroom for catching the morning sun. The step-down levels can break up the monotony of a large deck.

LINK UP THE LANDINGS

Linking decks with multiple landings helps break up an extended stairway and provides smaller activity areas. In this case, a slope that could have been unusable becomes an enticing path to the door with plenty of room for potted plants.

SMALL STEP-UPS

A series of small platforms bridges a natural rock formation close to the house. This approach allows the house to embrace the rugged site—another example of how it pays to work with nature and not against it. Additional decks off to the side and in back of the house let the homeowners take in the view from other angles.

LAKEFRONT LOOKOUT

This home suffered from a major challenge—the yard fell off so steeply to the water that it was essentially unusable. Now the deck takes the place of yard space, with the balcony providing a view of the outdoors as well as second-story access, while the main deck has plenty of space for family activities and large weekend gatherings.

CASCADING DECK

This gracefully designed and executed multilevel deck provides a variety of options for use. The top level—accessible from the master bedroom—supports a spa. Large platforms function both as stairs and small gathering spaces for entertaining large groups. The lower area provides a cozy place to sit and a transition to the patio and yard .

CLASSIC COLUMNS

Style is the key to this classic design, demonstrating that decks don't inherently have to look laid-back and casual. This design features two wraparound sections with separate access to each floor. The separate decks are positioned to make the most use of sun and shade patterns throughout the day.

Multiple and multilevel decks *(continued)*

CONTRASTING LEVELS.

Multilevel decks can be built as a series of independent decks linked with stairs. They can also be built with low platforms next to or under each other. In this efficient approach, some of the foundation and framing serves both levels. In the example at right, the upper level is constructed as an individual deck. Posts supporting the beam also support the ledger for the lower level. When building the framing, it often works out well to step levels down by the width of one joist. A 2×8 joist will provide a standard step rise and a 2×6 joist will result in a more gentle step. The lower level could be expanded or offset by shifting post locations. In this example, the lower level doesn't require a railing, which adds to the architectural contrast.

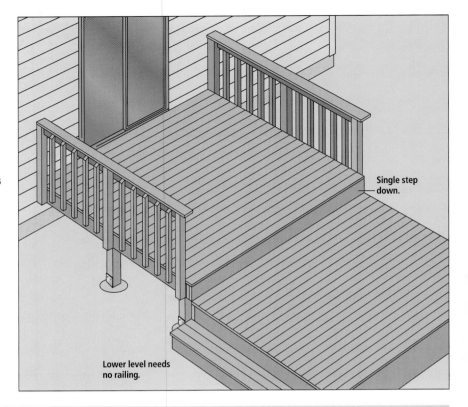

Single step down.

Lower level needs no railing.

LANDSCAPING ON MANY LEVELS.

Multilevel decks not only provide separate areas for different activities, they also increase your opportunities for landscaping. Permanent plantings (enclosed in a rough rock wall at the left side of the deck) go hand in hand with plants in containers on the deck.

If the landscape provides only enough room for one full-size deck, use the remaining space to install a platform walkup. Then fill in the unused areas with flowers and other accents.

STACKED FRAMES CHANGE LEVELS.

Stacked frames offer an easy way to change levels. Be sure to double the live load when computing beam spans and post spacing. Your decking pattern will determine the direction of the joists. If you want parallel decking on both sections, stack the frames with the joists parallel. If you want the decking in one section perpendicular to the other, hang the joists in one section perpendicular to the other. In either case, build the lower frame first and hang the joists, then hang the upper frame. Join the levels with metal connectors. A small-scale top frame will function as a simple step if you need one.

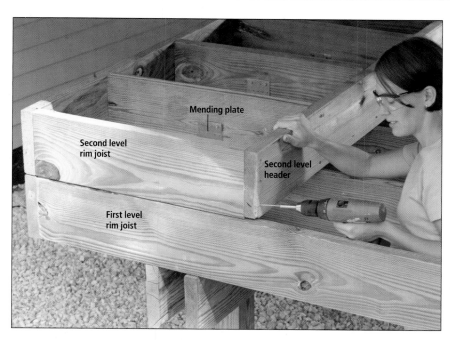

DOUBLE HEADER.

To extend a deck while creating a second level, you might be able to add framing to your existing deck foundation. If the new section is not too large or heavy (use span tables to compute loads, page 133), double the existing header and frame the extension from this point. Add a second-level frame over the first one that extends past the doubled header. This method can be used to frame a succession of gradual level changes.

BUILD INDIVIDUAL DECKS.

Sometimes building two or more individual decks is the best solution to raising levels. One level could be attached on one end to a ledger on the house, while the other could be freestanding. Lay out and construct each level with its own footings and framing. Treat each level as a single deck.

It's usually not a good idea to tie these decks together with screws or bolts: If one section settles differently than the other, the stress might crack the frames. If you need a level change more than a 2×6 or 2×8, link them with a step.

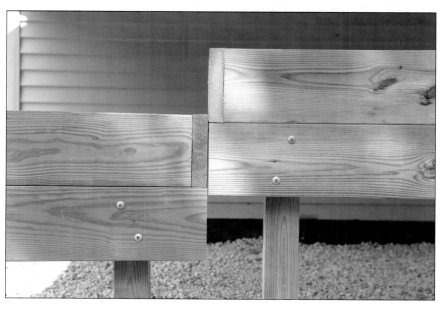

DESIGNING AN ENTRYWAY DECK

Decks are normally considered backyard structures for fun and sun. But decks are appropriate for front entries also, although they may require design refinements.

The entryway deck will probably be visible from the street, so you need to hide the foundation and framing with lattice, solid skirting, or well-designed planting beds. And while it's important to integrate a backyard deck into the overall design of your home, it's doubly important for a deck on the front of your home.

With a well-designed portico roof or other overhead structure, an entryway deck looks like an old-fashioned front porch. For entry stairs, consider adding risers to close up the back of the steps. Design your railing with special care.

∧

A CAREFUL UPDATE
Extending the entry, adding a side porch, and incorporating stylistic elements (including the solid skirt) appropriate to the house has updated this 1920s entry without conflicting with the house's Tudor lines.

∨

NO ADD-ONS HERE
A front-door deck may require more renovation so the new complements the old. The appropriate style of overhead structure with distinctive rafters and arches can do just that. This portico is not made for shade. Its real function is to enhance the entry without interfering with the sunlight.

ACCENT ON THE HORIZONTAL

Widening the stairway, adding a wide fascia to cover the joists, and installing a railing with aluminum balusters added a lot of space to this front-yard deck but still kept the emphasis on the basic horizontal character of the house. A coat of paint on the posts, deck frame, risers, and skirt works all the elements into a cohesive whole.

STAGING YOUR ENTRANCE

This graceful, gradually staged entryway deck is made of a series of platforms that ease the ascent to the doorway. The middle platform features a roomy built-in bench. Metal railings, common on entryways, help reinforce the deck's front entryway function. Landscaping plays a role too; hidden lights illuminate the pathway at night and tall bushes hide the structure of the platforms.

Designing an entryway deck *(continued)*

FANCIFUL FOURSQUARE
If attaching a deck to the house—either in front or in back—would destroy the lines that make the house so attractive, a detached deck might work. You don't need much space—a 10-foot octagon will provide enough space for family members to chat. A front-yard structure is more open to public view than a backyard deck, so build in privacy screens or make use of existing ones, like a high fence covered with vines..

WHEN A DECK IS NOT A DECK

Tradition says that porches are for the front of houses and decks are for the back. But the differences between a porch and a deck are largely theoretical. On older houses, porches are often partially enclosed and are usually fully integrated into the facade, sometimes even continuing the roof line of the house. That kind of design integration is important for a deck, too, so it doesn't seem like an afterthought.

ARTS-AND-CRAFTS
A deck can harmonize with any architectural style. How well it does that is, for the most part, up to the railing. Here, an arts-and-crafts stair railing leads up to a postwar bungalow. Lighted posts add safety and a warm design touch for evening hours.

Privacy makes a deck more pleasant and inviting. Without privacy, you're likely to feel uncomfortable on the deck, so it may go unused.

Block only the views that need blocking. Sometimes a deck-mounted structure is effective. Other times, on-deck screening will make you feel hemmed in. If so, move the privacy screen away from the deck.

The structures below can be built on the deck frame or as fences; construction methods are about the same: Posts and rails support screens or panels (the infill). Building a fence requires footings—laying out a fenceline is a lot like laying out the long side of a deck. You can usually modify an existing railing to accept siding. If you can't, remove the old infill and replace it.

SIDE-YARD SOLACE
What if your only available deck space is a narrow side yard too close to the neighbors? First design your deck to fit the space available. (Ground-level platforms adapt to almost any space.) Then build a privacy fence but leave openings so you won't feel walled in. Paint it bright and use modestly sized furniture.

Adding solid walls

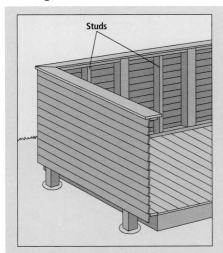

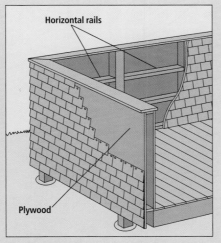

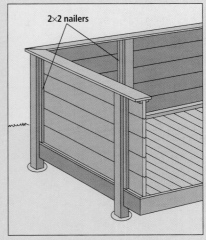

INSTALL HORIZONTAL SIDING,…

Clapboard or similar horizontal siding can be nailed to 2×4 studs if each bay is no more than 2 feet wide. To match the siding on the house, use the same exposure (the amount of siding depth that shows for each course).

…SHINGLES,…

Shingles on a deck can look great even if the house has a different type of siding. Install horizontal rails no more than 16 inches apart, and attach pressure-treated plywood. You can paint the shingles, stain and seal them, or just let them weather.

…OR TONGUE-AND-GROOVE BOARDS.

Solid tongue-and-groove boards look equally attractive from both sides of the deck. Install them centered on the posts with 1×1 or 2×2 nailers on the perimeter, as shown, or nail them to the outsides of the posts.

BUILDING FREESTANDING DECKS

A freestanding deck is a self supporting structure. It's not connected to the house, so it can go just about anywhere—out in the yard or right next to the house.

Why build a freestanding deck next to the house? If you want to construct two or three or more cascading platforms, it would save you the trouble of attaching ledgers to the house on three levels. Also, the construction of the house might not allow the needed ledgers.

A freestanding deck in a remote part of the yard can take advantage of a great view or the only private spot in the yard. Overlapping freestanding platforms can create a gradual stairway to the main deck.

A modular deck (opposite page) is the simplest of freestanding decks, and needs no foundation. In fact, free-standing decks often do not need footings at all. They are often built on precast piers—perhaps with shallow footings. A freestanding deck with piers won't be damaged by frost heave—all the piers or footings will rise and fall at the same time.

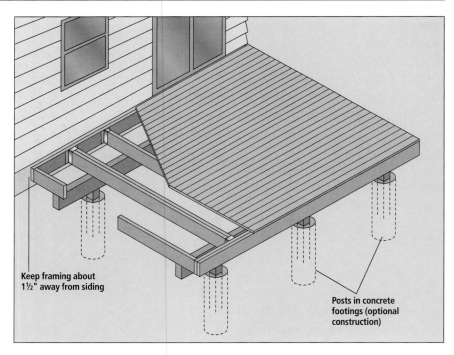

Keep framing about 1½" away from siding

Posts in concrete footings (optional construction)

CREATE AN INDEPENDENT FOUNDATION.

A freestanding deck is built in the same way as an attached deck, except that two (on long decks, more) footings and posts and an additional beam replace the ledger. These elements will increase your cost, time, and labor. Consider those factors when weighing design options for your deck.

REASONS FOR A FREESTANDING DECK

In areas where the soil is unstable, deck builders often build free-standing decks to avoid problems caused by uneven settling. Many professional deck builders design all their decks as freestanding units, because ledgers trap moisture, which can rot the deck and the house framing. Digging and pouring a few more footings may actually take less time (although it's more strenuous) than installing a ledger.

1 LAYOUT AND FRAMING.

Prepare the site, lay it out, then locate, pour, and dig footings. Bed piers or install posts and build the frame. Square the frame by measuring the diagonals. If piers are your only foundation, you may be able to avoid using batterboards. Assemble the frame, set it in the piers, and square it.

2 HANG JOISTS, LAY THE DECK.

Once you're certain the frame is square, keep it square by tacking 1×4 braces across two corners. Start installing the decking at the other end, keeping the boards spaced at ⅛ inch. When you reach the braces, remove them and finish the decking.

CREATING MODULAR DECKING

These simple panels, often called duckboards, are easy to build and can be combined into many shapes for an attractive parquet design. If you have a level yard and soil that does not get soggy, modular units can last a long time. And if you lay them on a firmly tamped bed of gravel, they will remain fairly stable.

If you are going to use modules in high-traffic areas or find that they have more spring to the step than you'd prefer, reinforce the center of each module with an extra 2×4 cleat.

USE MODULES TO FORM ANY PATTERN.

Modular construction is, by its nature, versatile and adaptable. You can use a modular approach to build a simple ground-level deck like the one above. You could lay out a larger deck or arrange modules as several decks joined by walkways. Modules could be laid around raised garden beds to create a boardwalk.

YOU'LL NEED

TIME: One hour to build the jig and about one hour for each module

SKILLS: Measuring, cutting, fastening

TOOLS: Basic carpentry tools

MIX AND MATCH MODULES.

You can probably think of several projects that could combine modular construction with standard deck-building techniques. Here, modules make a boardwalk from the house to a side deck—a great way to avoid the costs and labor of building a separate platform. If your needs or tastes change over the years, or if you simply want a change, just pick up the modules and rearrange them. You can stack them to make low steps. Alternate the direction of the decking for a parquet effect, as shown, or lay them in the same direction for continuous lines.

Creating modular decking *(continued)*

1 PREPARE THE SITE.

Use batter boards and mason's lines to outline the perimeter of the site, including a 3-inch sand border. Measure a 3–4–5 triangle (page 120) to square the corner, and stake the corners with a plumb bob. Run lines between the corner stakes and mark the outline on the ground (page 36). Remove the sod and soil to a depth of 5 inches. Spread 3 inches of gravel on the site, and level and tamp it. Then add 2 inches of sand, level, and tamp.

2 GANG-CUT THE BOARDS.

For each module, you will need 10 pressure-treated 2×4s, each 29 inches long. Cut them quickly by clamping several 2×4s edge to edge then cutting them in one pass with a circular saw. Use a straightedge to guide the saw.

SAVE THE SOD

Reuse the sod and top soil you remove from your deck site.
Before you excavate your deck site, take a look at areas in your yard that could use some sod patching. To make sod easier to reuse, cut it into strips with a spade, then work the spade under the sod and dislodge the roots. Roll the sod and water it after transplanting it. If you do throw the sod on the compost pile, put the grass side down to stop the it from growing. Add the top soil to garden beds.

3 BUILD A JIG.

To produce identical modules, make this jig from pressure-treated 2×4s about 3 feet long. Make sure that the inside edges are straight, then fasten the boards at the corners to leave a 29×29-inch inside framing area.

Align the corners with a framing square as you fasten the boards together. The jig doesn't have cross bracing, so check it for square after assembling each module.

④ BUILD THE MODULES.

Set the jig on a solid, flat surface, then tack a 2×2 guide on one side to keep the ends lined up. Each module requires eight 2×4 deck boards and two 2×4 cleats. Set the cleats on edge at the sides of the jig, as shown.

Attach the decking with 2½-inch decking screws. Space the boards at ⅛ inch. The width of 2×4s varies, so you may need to adjust the spacing to make the last piece even with the cleat.

⑤ SET THE MODULES.

Lay the modules on the sand bed, alternating the direction of the boards. Attach modules to each other by drilling pilot holes and toenailing, as shown.

⑥ TRIM THE EDGES.

Once you have assembled the modules in a pattern, you may want to trim the edges for a more finished look. Cut two 1×4s to fit flush on opposite ends and two others for the edges .

You may have to remove some sand so you can fasten the trim flush with the decking. Replace the sand and tamp around the edges.

WOOD PATH

Modules make a boardwalk.
Building and installing deck modules is easier than pouring a concrete walkway or laying a brick sidewalk. A boardwalk can connect the house to the garage or the house to a modular deck. Enlarge the jig shown on the opposite page to build a 36-inch (or wider) path. Larger modules will require additional cleats in the center. By excavating, you can set the modules level with the grade.

Wood and water make perfect companions, perhaps because of their mutual natural origins. A deck surface surrounding a pool does more than enhance the looks of the whole. It's a surface that will withstand years of use—making a spa, hot tub, or swimming pool a natural long-term partner for a deck.

To get to that point, you'll need to make special preparations. The water in a spa, hot tub, or pool will weigh a ton or more, and local building codes will probably require a ground-level reinforced concrete pad (see the photograph, opposite).

The pool will require an opening in the deck, so you'll need special framing. (See the illustration on the opposite page).

The amount of space required depends on the size of the hot tub or spa. You probably won't need a large deck, however. Small spas can fit quite easily on a 12×12-foot surface. You'll want privacy, of course, and shade, so put the deck out of sight, or plan effective screening.

Pools and hot tubs require plumbing and electrical connections, too. Hide these systems behind framing or skirting. Build pull-out or hinged hatches into the decking or make skirting sections removable for repairs and maintenance.

Code requirements for fencing around pools and spas are strict—access to the location usually has to be childproof. With careful planning, you may be able to combine the required fencing with a railing system on the deck.

RAISE THE SPA.

A spa or hot tub can provide a striking visual accent if you raise its liner and frame above the deck surface. This construction also gives you a chance to add some built-in seating. With a raised unit, you can sit down without having to dangle your feet in the water. Raised water features can sit on a concrete pad or substantial framing set on posts and footings. Don't begin planning without consulting with your local building code officials.

DROP IN A TUB.

Setting a spa or hot tub flush with the deck surface makes it easy for you to sit on the edge with your feet in the water. However, the rim of the unit will not support the weight of the spa. That support comes from framing on posts or a concrete pad underneath. Safety is a primary concern because children and adults can easily fall in. A sturdy cover and adequate supervision are musts.

BUILDING AN ELEVATED PAD.

Build an elevated pad following the same techniques as for a ground-level pad—laying out the site with batterboards, building and staking forms, and pouring the concrete (page 56). But for this foundation, you should order concrete delivery from a ready-mix truck. An elevated pad for a spa or hot tub can easily require 15 cubic feet or more of concrete—a volume that's impractical to mix by hand.

MAKING DESIGN CHOICES.

Commercial suppliers offer a wide array of spas and hot tubs that can be installed on (or in) a deck. To choose one, first decide the general theme of your deck design, then determine the general location of the spa. Find one that fits—both structurally and visually—then round out your design and your dimensioned plans with the spa as the central focal point.

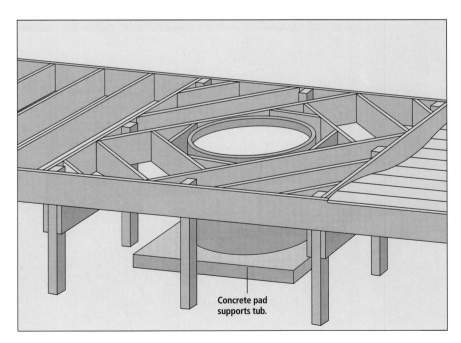

Concrete pad supports tub.

FRAMING A TUB SURROUND.

A recessed water feature can never have any part of its weight borne by its rim. You have to center the opening in the framing exactly above the supporting pad. Begin by building the pad a little larger than the minimum dimensions specified by the manufacturer. That will allow you to adjust the framing slightly from one side to the other in case on-site measurements don't quite match your dimensioned plan. Then block the framing so it supports all the edges of the decking.

DESIGNING ELEVATED DECKS

People often build houses on steep slopes because of the spectacular views. But the slope may make the yard largely unusable. An elevated deck can solve that problem.

Supported on posts that reach to the main level of the house (or its second story), an elevated deck adds outdoor living space that might otherwise be available only with extensive grading. Flattening or terracing a sloped yard can cause extensive and expensive landscaping problems. An elevated deck might provide an easier solution by bringing the outside surface up to the house.

A deck can also have two stories or rise to nearly any height, such as a private sun room or balcony off an upstairs bedroom.

The tall posts, however, create design challenges because the taller they are, the more spindly they look. Use thicker posts than codes require, or add trim to smaller posts to make them look more massive. Cover any bracing that codes require with a skirt or plantings.

LET THE LIGHT IN
One benefit of an elevated deck is the increased light it lets into the adjacent rooms. Access to the outdoors and increased natural light are highly sought by remodelers. An elevated deck can meet both requirements, but it can also shade lower level rooms dramatically. If you only need sitting space in your second-story spot, scale the deck back to about 8 feet wide to avoid putting the first floor rooms in the dark.

CAUTION

HIGH ALERT

Building an elevated deck can be difficult, even dangerous. Large posts and beams are heavy, and working with them 10 or 20 feet up can be risky. A tall elevated deck is a job only for a skilled, knowledgeable builder with skilled help and adequate ladders or scaffolding.

SPLIT-LEVEL ELEVATION
If you build an elevated deck, consider adding an intermediate level at the same time, even if your plans don't include a stairway to the ground. The lower deck shares the same footings and posts, so extra costs are minimal. And you can screen the lower level to make space you can use in different kinds of weather.

IT'S IN THE DETAILS
An elevated deck such as this one should be designed with the appearance of the exposed structural members in mind. This example has decorative lattice arches between support posts to incorporate them into the overall design.

LAYERING ALONG THE LAKEFRONT
Sometimes a site is too steep or shallow for a stairway to the surrounding yard. Several flights of stairs with landings between can overcome the problem. Broaden the idea by creating a series of stairs with activity areas along the way. This deck features a dining spot and a pool area with a built-in bench.

Designing elevated decks *(continued)*

HOW HIGH CAN YOUR DECK GO? (MAXIMUM POST HEIGHT)

Post size	Load area (joist span × beam span)						
	36	48	60	72	84	96	108
4×4	10'	9'	8'	7'	6'	5'	
4×6	14'	12'	11'	10'	9'	8'	7'
6×6	17'	16'	15'	14'	13'	12'	

This table shows maximum post height for Southern pine and Douglas fir (graded No. 2 and Better), the most commonly available species of pressure-treated lumber.

To determine the post height for your deck, first compute its load area by multiplying the joist span (the distance between beams or between the beam and the ledger) times the beam span (the distance between posts). The result is the square footage of your load area.

For example, if your deck has joists spanning 8 feet and a beam spanning 6 feet between posts, the load area on the deck equals 48. Following the appropriate column in the table, you'll see that you can use 4×4 posts up to 9 feet tall. If your deck has a higher elevation, use larger posts.

(See page 133 for more on joist and beam spans.)

The sizing on this table will satisfy most building departments, but check with your local inspector before you start work. You can always use larger posts than are required. On elevated decks, 6×6 posts often look better than 4×4s, even if they aren't needed for strength.

SAFE HEIGHTS

- The maximum acceptable height of posts you can use on a given deck depends on several factors, including the size of the post, the species of the wood and its quality, the sizes and spans of joists and beams, and local building codes and regulations.

- Higher decks might require larger posts or closer spacing, as well as larger footings.

- If the posts also will support a large overhead structure, check with a design professional or your local building department about the post size to use.

MORE OF EVERYTHING.

In addition to taller posts, an elevated deck can require more footings, concrete, and bracing. Other than the size of the materials, construction methods and sequence are the same as for lower decks.

BRACING TALL POSTS

Building codes in many areas—especially where loose soil, earthquakes, or periodic high winds are problems—require post bracing on decks with posts taller than 5 feet. Even if your area doesn't have those problems, bracing can make your deck more stable.

Most bracing can be made with 2×4s, but for braces more than 8 feet long, use 2×6s. Secure braces with ⅜-inch lag screws with washers, or carriage bolts with nuts and washers.

Freestanding decks should be braced if they are more than 3 feet above ground. If you don't like the appearance of the exposed braces, add skirting to the posts.

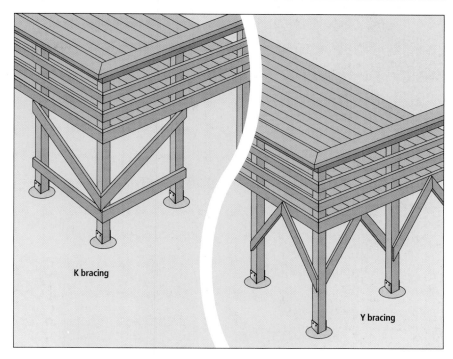

K bracing

Y bracing

THE ALPHABET OF BRACES.

Bracing styles are often named after the letters they suggest. The most common types are K and Y (above) and X and W (below) bracing. The strongest bracing ties posts to the beams. The style of bracing you employ may depend on appearance and how accessible you want the space beneath the deck to be. But looks may not be everything—building codes may dictate what style you use. To help prevent rot and for neater appearance, miter the joints. When two braces meet on a post, leave a small gap between them to allow for drainage.

4x4 spacer

SPACING THE BRACE.

X bracing or any other style which mounts braces on opposite sides of the posts will create a space where the braces cross each other. Fill the space and increase strength with a spacer the same size as your posts.

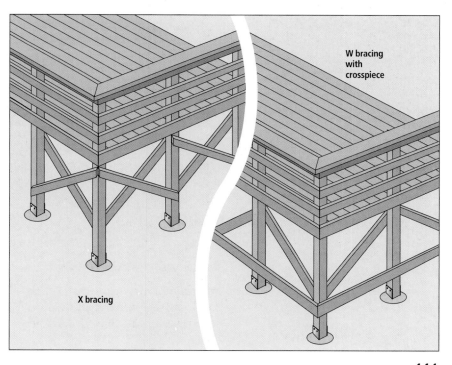

W bracing with crosspiece

X bracing

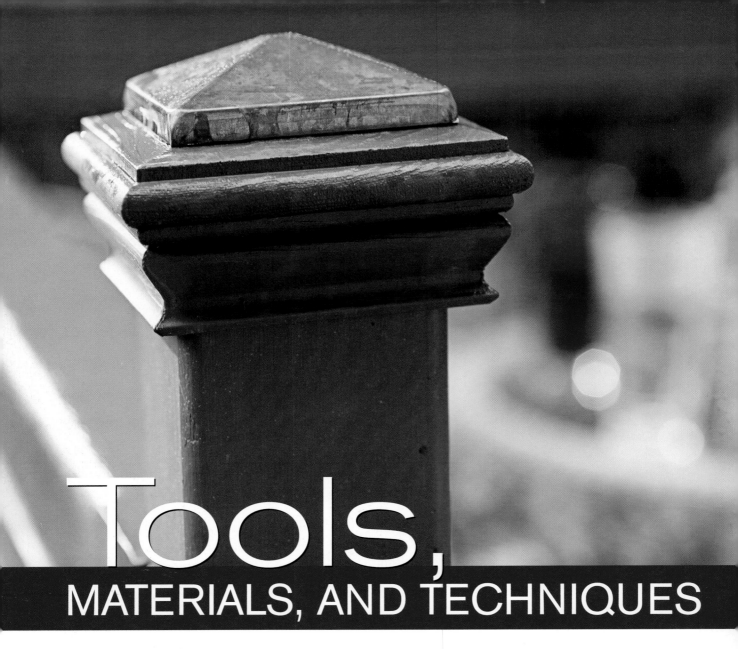

Tools,
MATERIALS, AND TECHNIQUES

Building a deck requires only a basic set of tools (you may already have most of them), some understanding of lumber and other materials, and fundamental carpentry skills. If you're a newcomer to home-remodeling, you're short a few tools, or you lack expertise in wood species or construction techniques, you can still do the job. You can buy or rent the tools you'll need, and you'll learn a lot about wood and carpentry as you plan the project. If you buy tools, get the best ones you can afford—they will be useful in later projects. Rent tools that you're not likely to need in the future. You'll find enough information in this chapter to make the right choices about tools and lumber. And you can always ask the home-center staff for information on materials and fasteners. Many employees in do-it-yourself retail outlets have built projects themselves. And if you're just starting out, or your skills are rusty, practice the techniques shown in this chapter before you start building.

IT'S ALL IN THE DETAILS
Finishing touches such as this copper post cap contribute to the overall effect of your deck. Consider the choices for materials—from decking to rails to fasteners—as you plan your deck project. Select those that meet your budget, fit your project needs, and contribute to a finished deck you will enjoy for years.

GOING CORDLESS
You'll need a power drill to drill holes and drive screws, but which one, corded or cordless? A cordless drill (with enough power and a back-up battery) is a better choice for most chores. A variable-speed cordless drill/driver makes short work of screwing down decking.

STANDARD TOOLS, NEW MATERIALS
Conventional tools such as this circular saw work well for cutting lumber and composite decking. See pages 122–123 to learn the proper techniques for using a circular saw. See pages 130–132 for information about selecting lumber and composite materials.

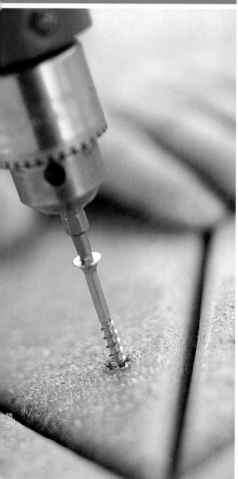

CAUTION

WORK-SITE SAFETY

Work-site safety means following guidelines and exercising common sense. Hand tools can hurt you, and power tools used improperly can be downright dangerous. But there's no reason to fear them if you follow these guidelines:

■ Use tools only for the tasks they were designed for. If a tool came with an instruction manual, take the time to read it to find out what the tool can do and what it can't do.

■ Check on the condition of a tool before using it. A dull cutting blade or a loose hammer head, for example, can be dangerous. Also inspect the cord of a power tool to make sure it's not damaged.

■ Don't work with tools if you're tired or in a hurry.

■ Don't work with tools if you have been drinking alcoholic beverages that day.

■ Wear safety goggles, a dust mask, ear protectors, gloves, and work shoes or boots when appropriate for the task.

■ The safety mechanisms on power tools are there for your protection. Do not tamper with or remove them from the tool.

■ Do not wear loose-fitting clothes or dangling jewelry while you are using tools.

■ Keep other people, especially children, at a safe distance.

ESSENTIAL TOOLS

You may already have all of the tools you'll need to build your deck.

Compare the tools you have with the tools shown here; add the tools you don't have. Most of them will be handy to have long after the deck is finished, so buy high-quality tools. Avoid bargain-priced tools, which often break, wear out quickly, don't stay sharp, and may be less comfortable to use.

Layout tools

Layout can be the most exacting aspect of deck building, but layout tools aren't expensive. Here's what you'll need.

Line level: This small level hooks to mason's line that can be stretched over distances too long to span with a carpenter's level.

Mason's line: The mainstay of layout work. Use nylon; it doesn't stretch.

Steel tape: This is a do-it-yourselfer's constant companion. A 1-inch blade will extend farther without sagging. You'll need a 16-footer—a 25-footer will save you time.

Plumb bob: This indicates vertical and helps mark post-hole locations.

Carpentry tools

These tools are the backbone of do-it-yourself carpentry. If you're assembling your tool chest for the first time, buy high-quality tools; you'll use them for other projects. You may not appreciate the many uses for the tools until you own them.

Adjustable clamp: Handy for holding thick pieces of lumber. Buy several.

Adjustable wrench: Use this to fasten nuts, bolts, and lag screws, or to hold a machine-bolt head while you tighten the nut with a socket wrench.

C clamp: These clamps come in a variety of sizes and handle many jobs. Never buy just one of any clamp.

Carpenter's level: Get a 48-inch model for plumbing and leveling. Shorter versions may give false readings over long spans. Buy one with a rigid steel or aluminum frame.

Carpenter's pencil: To avoid endless sharpening and to make visible lines, use a chisel-pointed carpenter's pencil. Buy a sharpener too.

Cat's paw: Makes pulling nails easier.

Caulking gun: Dispenses caulk from tubes for sealing ledgers and other joints that need to be waterproof.

Chalk line and chalk: You'll need these to snap straight lines for cuts.

Chisel: Essential for cleaning out notches. Buy high-quality chisels and take good care of them. Drive wood-handled chisels with a mallet, not a metal hammer. Sharp chisels make clean, accurate cuts. Poorly fitting notches make weak joints.

Circular saw: These come in different sizes. Get a heavy-duty saw with a 7¼-inch carbide-tipped combination blade. The extra power will come in handy on this or any other project that requires cutting of framing members.

Circular saw · Plane · Cordless drill · Slip-joint pliers · Line level · Steel tape · Framing square · Plumb bob · Handsaw · Mason's line · Chalk Line · Torpedo Level · Utility knife · Pry bar · Caulking gun · Cat's paw · Carpenter's pencil · Post level · Locking pliers · Adjustable wrench · Socket wrench

Carpenter's level

Water level

Nail set

C clamp

Power drill

T-bevel

Combination square

Framing hammer

Chisel

Adjustable clamp

Sawhorses

Layout square

Squeeze clamps

Jigsaw

Combination square: This is an indispensable tool. It helps you check 90- and 45-degree angles quickly, measure depth from surfaces, and lay out cutting lines.

Cordless drill: This essential tool drills holes and easily drives screws. Buy at least a 14.4-volt model with a spare battery. You'll need spade bits of appropriate sizes for larger holes and to start mortises. Twist drills will drill holes up to ½-inch diameter for screws and bolts.

Framing hammer: Buy a high-quality, 20-ounce hammer. The extra weight may seem tiring at first, but you'll appreciate it after driving a deckful of 10d nails.

Framing square: You'll use this large square to square corners and to mark stair stringers.

Handsaw : You'll need this for quick cuts and to finish some corner cuts where a circular saw won't go.

Jigsaw: If you're cutting any fancy

patterns, you'll need one of these. (Buy a heavy-duty model.)

Layout square: This triangular square helps you to quickly figure angled cuts or mark cut lines. It's tough and compact, and will hold its shape after getting banged around. Some carpenters use this square to guide circular-saw cuts.

Locking pliers: This handy, versatile tool holds, grips, and clamps.

Nail set: Use for setting finishing nails in railings or trim.

Plane: Use this tool to shave wood off the edge of a board or round sharp edges on a post or railing.

Post level: This is a one-purpose tool, but nothing does it better. Strap it to a post to plumb two sides at once.

Power drill: A variable speed, reversible corded drill is handy for drilling holes in heavy framing.

Pry bar: This is handy when you need to force a warped board into place or to remove nails.

Sawhorses: You'll need these to support lumber for cutting.

Slip-lock pliers: Pliers are handy for gripping, holding, and pulling.

Socket wrench: A ratchet handle and socket is the best tool for tightening nuts and lag screws.

Squeeze clamps: Inexpensive and quick to use, these are less likely to dent lumber.

T-bevel: This gauge adjusts to duplicate an angle.

Torpedo level: This short level fits in tighter spaces when a carpenter's level is too long.

Utility knife: With a retractable blade, this knife will sharpen your pencils and trim some materials.

Water level: This device makes long-distance leveling easy and accurate. Some models attach to the ends of your garden hose.

SPECIALIZED TOOLS

Sometimes the most difficult and costly decision you have to make on a project is which, if any, new tools to buy. That's especially true of some of the specialized tools shown on this page.

These are tools you might not use much after your deck is done. For example, if you think you might need a power nailer or hammer drill only a couple of times in the next 10 years, you're better off renting them.

Many do-it-yourselfers like to look at a project as an opportunity to add new tools to their collection. But remember that needing a tool doesn't always mean you have to buy it.

Framing tools

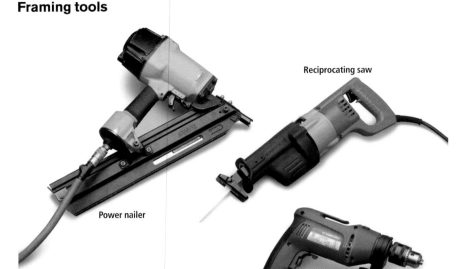

Power nailer

Reciprocating saw

Hammer drill

Hammer drill: Its dual drilling and hammering action makes drilling holes in masonry easy. This is handy if you need to install a ledger on masonry or set post bases.

Power nailer: Rent this for framing and attaching deck boards.
Reciprocating saw: This is a useful tool for demolition and is ideal for cutting posts.

RENTING TOOLS

When you need an expensive tool for only a short period, or if you can't afford to buy it new, visit a tool rental store. A reasonably well-equipped rental store will carry any tool you find in this book, including circular saws and drills.

When planning tool purchases, it pays to compare the costs of buying new versus renting.

Tools are rented by the hour, day, or week. To avoid excessive charges, don't pick up the tool until you need it. Clean the tool before returning to avoid extra charges.

FRAMING NAILER.

This is a standard tool for the pros. Push the safety lock shoe against the work and pull the trigger. The lock prevents the gun from accidentally discharging the nail.

RECIPROCATING SAW.

The saw blade moves back and forth, and that can make the saw jump. Steady the saw with the shoe against the stock and keep it there until you've cut completely through.

Tools for excavating and concrete

Round-nose shovel · Clamshell digger · Garden rake · Hoe · Spade · Tamping bar · Wheelbarrow

Shovels: Excavate with a round-nose shovel, remove sod with a spade.
Garden rake: This is for leveling soil and smoothing gravel.
Clamshell digger: Its hinged blades dig clean, straight-sided holes.
Tamping bar: This tamps soil.
Wheelbarrow: Mix concrete in it.
Hoe: Get a mason's hoe. It has holes that make mixing easier.

Power post holes

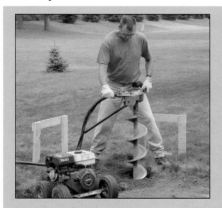

A ONE-PERSON POWER AUGER.

You'll need a trailer to haul some models home. Start the engine. Set the bit over the hole, and lower it slowly, letting its weight do the work. Raise the bit periodically to clean it. Keep the bit turning when raising it from the hole. Add extensions for deeper holes.

A TWO PERSON POWER AUGER.

Two-person motorized augers are more difficult to operate. Get detailed instructions when renting one. The torque they produce can knock you off balance. Start the engine, and plant your (and your helper's) feet firmly before engaging the bit. Be braced for roots and rocks.

A TRAILER-MOUNTED POWER AUGER.

This hydraulically-powered unit produces maximum boring power with minimum wear and tear on the operator. To ease the auger into the soil, you simply operate a control handle. The hydraulics of the unit do the lifting and lowering.

MEASURING AND MARKING

Accurate measuring and marking are essential to successful carpentry. A mistake in measuring usually results in wasted time and material. Although it may seem simple, developing accurate measuring skills takes practice.

Don't rush your measurements; double-check them. Apply the carpenters' maxim, "Measure twice, cut once."

No matter what measuring device you use, become familiar with it and learn how to read it accurately. Learn to immediately recognize the ¼-inch and the ⅛-inch increments. Many a board has been ruined because the carpenter misread the mark. Once you've made a measurement, jot it down on paper, a wood scrap, or the board itself.

A blade that has ¹⁄₃₂-inch marks for the first few inches is not essential; Sometimes those tiny increments can be distracting. Carpentry rarely calls for precision greater than ¹⁄₁₆ inch. That's because it's very difficult to cut more precisely than that with a circular saw.

Sometime it's not measuring that introduces an error—it's the marking. Make a clear mark with a sharp No. 2 pencil, the thin edge of a sharpened carpenter's pencil, a knife, or a scratch awl.

USE A SINGLE TAPE

Different measuring tapes sometimes disagree, and may vary by as much as ⅛ inch. This can lead to frustration, especially when working with a partner who is using his or her own tape. Before you start measuring and cutting, compare the tapes to be sure they're calibrated exactly the same.

TAKE AN OUTSIDE MEASUREMENT.

To take an outside measurement, hook the tape over the outside edge of the board. Make sure you have engaged the board with the tang of the hook and not the rivets that hold it in place. Pull the case of the tape toward the point you want to measure. Set the blade of the tape against the outside point and read the tape where it intersects the edge. Mark the measurement or write it on a piece of scrap.

TAKE AN INSIDE MEASUREMENT.

To measure the space between framing members, first hook the tape over the outside edge of one of the boards (or run it out by hand) as if you were taking an outside measurement. Pull the case just past the point you wish to measure and lock the blade. Then lift the hook off the board and push it gently on the edge of the inside face of the board. Read the tape where the inside face of the other board intersects it.

Marking cross cuts

V marks the spot

1 MEASURE THE LENGTH.

Extend the tape from the squared end of the board to the point where you will make the cut. Mark that point with a V, not a single line.

Layout square

X marks waste side

2 EXTEND THE MARK.

Hold the point of your pencil on the mark and slide a layout square along the edge of the board until it touches the pencil tip. Run your pencil along the square.

Marking rip cuts

Measure the width of the cut on both ends of the board, then snap a chalk line between the marks or use a straightedge to connect them with a pencil line.

Marking miter cuts

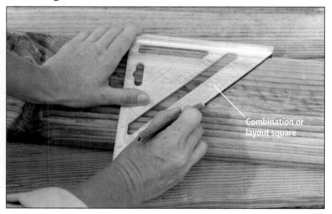

Combination or layout square

Set a square flush against the edge of the board at the point you wish to cut. (When marking the end of a board, pull the the edge of the square down slightly from the corner.) Hold it steady and mark the line.

Mark the intersection of the boards.

Marking on site

On-site measurements are usually more accurate than those taken with tapes. Whenever possible, hold the board to be cut in position, then mark the cutline.

All carpentry projects have elements that must be square, plumb, or level. These characteristics are not only important because they improve the appearance of a structure, but because they also increase its structural integrity. A deck that is not square, plumb, and level may collapse.

Depending on what part of the project is involved, you can make sure your construction meets these criteria with a variety of tools. Most of them aren't complicated, but you should treat them with care.

If the edge on a combination square is damaged or worn, you won't get a square reading. The same holds true for a bent or worn framing square. If the vials in your level get knocked out of alignment, your level won't level. Check squares against a known 90-degree corner (the factory corner of a 4×8 sheet of plywood, for example). Test a level by leveling a board with it, then turning the level around. It should show level both ways. If you can't repair or adjust an inaccurate tool, buy a new one before you get started.

THE MULTIPURPOSE LAYOUT SQUARE

Almost every carpenter's belt has a hammer, utility knife, pencil, and the ever-handy layout square. With a triangular layout square, you can quickly mark 45- and 90-degree angles simply by holding the square with its body firmly against a factory edge. Other angles are stamped on the body of the square and can be used with a fair degree of accuracy. In addition, the layout square is a handy guide for cutting with a circular saw (see page 123).

FRAMING SQUARE.

Use a framing square to square large corners—the header and rim joist, for example. Place the square inside or outside the corner and look along the lengths of both the tongue (short side) and the blade (long side). They should fit flush against the boards along their entire lengths. If you see light, adjust the boards until the square fits snugly. Don't be satisfied if only the corner of the square is tight. The framing is not true unless the square fits snugly along the entire lengths of the tongue and blade.

3-4-5 TRIANGLE.

This method is handy when laying out sites or when working with corners too large for a framing square. Measure out 3 feet on one side of the corner, and mark the measurement precisely with tape. Measure out 4 feet on the other side and mark it also. Have a helper to hold the end of a tape measure on one mark, then measure to the other. If the distance between them is 5 feet, the corner is square. If it's not, adjust the corner and measure again. Multiples of 3, 4, and 5 feet are even more accurate.

Mark square line and trim the end.

CHECK BOARD ENDS FOR SQUARE.

Careful measuring will be wasted on a piece of lumber that is not square; one edge will be longer than the other. Check the end of the board end by holding a combination or layout square firmly against a factory edge. If the end isn't square, mark a square line and trim the board.

EXTENDING A SQUARE LINE.

Some installations require extending a level or square line to other faces of a board. A combination square or layout square will help you do this quickly. Slide the square on an unmarked face until it reaches the level line you've marked already. Transfer this line to the unmarked face and repeat for other faces.

USE A POST LEVEL.

Deck posts must be plumb in two planes at the same time. You can plumb them one side at a time with a carpenter's level, but a post level, with its two vials, plumbs both sides at once. Strap or hold the level on the post and brace the post when the bubbles in both vials are centered.

LONG-DISTANCE LEVELING.

When you need to mark or extend a level line over more than 6 feet, use a water level or use a level on a straight board.

A water level uses the principle that water will find the same level over any distance. Two pieces of clear plastic tubing fastened to the ends of a hose let you see the water at both ends. Hold the ends of the level against both surfaces and mark the boards at the waterline.

You can also set (or better yet, tape) a carpenter's level to a straight board to extend a level line. Hold the board against the line at one end, adjust the board to center the bubble in the vial, and mark the other end. Using this method is easier if you have someone to help.

PLUMBING WITH A LEVEL.

A carpenter's level has vials at each end set perpendicular to its frame. Use these vials for plumbing a board when no other method will work—when plumbing the face of a ledger, for example. Hold the level vertically against the board and adjust the board until the bubble in the end vial (the top one) is centered.

CUTTING WITH A CIRCULAR SAW

Circular saws are so versatile and convenient that it's hard to imagine building a deck without one. Today's saws are lightweight and relatively inexpensive, and double insulation reduces the danger of electric shock.

You will probably cut most of your deck lumber with a circular saw. Whether crosscutting 1× stock, ripping plywood, or cutting bricks with a masonry blade, you'll do the job better if you follow a few basic rules when using this tool.

Allow the saw to reach full operating speed away from the wood, then slowly push the blade into the wood. Some carpenters look at the blade as they cut; others rely on the gunsight notch. Choose the method that's most comfortable for you. Don't let the blade wander—find the straight path and push the saw through the wood smoothly. You'll need some practice before you can do this consistently.

SUPPORT THE MATERIAL.

Well-supported work results in clean, safe cuts. Support the board so the saw won't bind or kick back and to keep the end of the board from splintering as the waste falls away. If the waste piece is short, support just the good end of the board. If the waste end is longer than 2 feet, support the board in four places so neither end of the board will bind the blade and you can make a straight, neat cut. Support the lumber in four places for best results on all cuts.

CHOOSING A CIRCULAR SAW AND BLADES

Choose a comfortable saw.
It should have some heft (and draw about 15 amps of power), but should not be so heavy that it is difficult to maneuver. You should be able to see the blade and gunsight notch easily. Depth and bevel adjustments should move easily and stay put.

If you buy only one blade for a circular saw, choose a carbide-tipped combination blade with at least 24 teeth. It works well for rough work and makes crosscuts and rip cuts clean enough for most finish work. For finer work, such as cutting cap-rail miters, buy a blade with 40 or more teeth.

CAUTION

AVOIDING KICKBACK

It can happen to even the most experienced carpenter: The blade binds, causing the saw to jump backward. That's called kickback, and it can mar the lumber you are working on or cause injury as you lose control of the saw. Unsupported stock often is the problem, but these are some other possibilities: A dull blade will bind and kick the saw back. Change your blade or get it sharpened if you have to push hard to make it cut. Bent or twisted lumber will grab a blade. Sheets of plywood are particularly prone to bending while being cut. Make sure your stock is evenly supported. Kickback also can occur when you back the saw up while cutting or when you try to cut a turn. If your saw gets off line, stop it, back up, and start again. Occasionally, certain wood grains will grab the blade and cause kickback. The only thing you can do about this is be prepared for it.

Don't wear loose sleeves and don't get your face near the saw, trying to see a line, for example.

SET THE BLADE DEPTH

Before you make a cut, set the blade to extend no more than ¼ inch past the thickness of the wood. (Be sure to unplug the saw before you do this.) Release the saw plate latch to position the plate to the proper depth.

This may seem like a lot of bother, especially if you are frequently switching between cutting 1× and 2× lumber. But it's worth the trouble because a saw blade that extends only slightly below the material will produce a much cleaner cut than a blade that extends way below the material.

The deeper the blade is set, the more prone it will be to binding and kickback, endangering the work and your safety.

SQUARE THE BLADE.

Even on a brand new, factory-set saw, the blade may not be square to the saw plate. That will produce beveled cuts. To square the blade, unplug the saw, hold a layout or try square against the blade (between the teeth) and the plate, and adjust the plate until you can't see light between the blade and the square.

ALIGN THE BLADE WITH THE CUT LINE.

Once you have drawn an accurate cutoff line and have properly supported the board, position the saw blade on the scrap side of the line. The teeth on most circular saw blades are offset in an alternating pattern, half to the left and half to the right. When clamping a guide, align a tooth that points toward the cutoff line.

GUIDE THE CUT WITH A SQUARE.

With practice, you will learn to cut accurately without a guide. For now, and for precise cuts, guide the cut with a square. For 90-degree cuts, a layout square works well because its heel plate keeps it stable. Line up the blade with the cut, then slide the square up against the saw plate. Hold the board and the square with your free hand to keep them steady.

OTHER GUIDES FOR MITERS.

With care, you can improvise a saw guide that will be as accurate as a miter box. Set a T-bevel to the correct angle and transfer the angle to the board.

Clamp a straight piece of 1× stock parallel to the cut line and at a distance that will put the saw blade just on the waste side of the cut line. It may take some experimenting before you get everything to line up

properly. Measure the distance from the blade to the edge of the saw plate (many come from the factory already marked). Use this to mark your parallel line for the guide.

For long rip cuts, clamp the factory edge of a 1× board or a drywall square to the material, setting it back from the cut line to allow for the width of the saw plate.

DRILLING

The electric drill (with a cord or cordless) is today's preferred tool for drilling holes; you won't see many carpenters using a brace and bit. In fact, the cordless drill can help with so many tasks that it ranks as everyone's basic power tool. With a variable-speed reversible drill/driver, you can drill a hole of about any size, drive screws into wood or metal, buff and grind, and even mix paint.

A drill is not as dangerous as a circular saw, of course, but you still need to keep safety in mind as you use it. Always wear safety goggles (the kind with side protectors) when you are drilling. Insert the bit or accessory fully into the chuck and tighten the chuck jaws firmly. Clamp the workpiece if you can—the bit can bind and cause a piece to spin, causing injury. Don't force the drill; allow its speed to do the work.

CHOOSING A DRILL

■ Avoid buying a low-quality power drill or any model with a ¼-inch chuck.

■ A cordless drill can make your work easier, but only if it is powerful enough to do most things that a corded drill can do. Any cordless drill under 14.4 volts probably won't have the power you need. An 18-volt model is better. Get two batteries for any cordless drill.

■ A drill with a ⅜-inch chuck is ideal for most household tasks (including building a deck). Larger drills will have more power, but they're harder to handle and you'll rarely need that power.

■ Buy a variable-speed, reversible drill. Tasks often require variable drilling speeds and reversing capability. Most high-quality models have both.

■ A keyless chuck is a great time saver that allows you to tighten the bit in the chuck by twisting its nose. Do a little research on this feature; some keyless chucks hold bits better than others.

■ Get a model with a two-speed transmission—one for drilling and the other for driving screws.

■ A hammer drill combines the rotary action of a drill with the percussive action of a hammer. It's the best kind for drilling concrete and masonry.

MAKE A STARTING MARK.

Twist drills tend to skate off your center mark when they begin turning, so give them a starting dimple with an awl or a center punch. Set the tip of the bit into the punch mark, start the drill slowly, and increase the speed as it bites into the wood.

KEEP CHIPS FROM CLOGGING HOLES.

When you drill deep holes into thick material, wood chips build up in the hole, which can clog the bit and cause it to bind. Don't force the bit. Instead, withdraw the bit from the hole frequently while the drill is running. This will pull trapped wood chips to the surface. If you're working with sappy or moist wood, shavings may clog the flute of the bit. If this happens, withdraw the drill and stop it. Then clean out the flute with the tip of a nail. If the bit jams, reverse the drill rotation and pull the bit straight out.

IMPROVISE A GUIDE.

Most holes are drilled perpendicular to the surface of the wood. You can easily help keep the bit square by clamping a piece of scrap next to the hole. Start the bit in the hole, then move the scrap to it and clamp it.

When you need to drill a hole at an angle, make a guide by cutting a piece of scrap to the same angle.

Clamp the guide so it aligns the tip of the bit exactly on your center mark. Begin by drilling perpendicular to the surface. Once you have gone deep enough to keep the bit from skating away, shift the drill to the angle.

DRILLING MASONRY AND CONCRETE

Use a masonry bit when drilling into brick or concrete. Check the bit often to make sure it's not overheating. If you see smoke, stop immediately.

Here is a trick that works surprisingly well: Spray the bit and the hole with window cleaner as you work. This keeps the bit cool, and the foaming of the cleaner helps bring debris out of the hole.

When drilling into concrete, you may run into an especially hard spot (usually a rock embedded in the concrete). Take the bit out, insert a masonry nail or thin cold chisel, and with a hammer, crack the rock. That will give your bit a place to grab. If you have a lot masonry drilling to do, buy or rent a hammer drill.

DOUBLE DRILL BOLT HOLES

A spade bit tears the wood as it drills through the back side. For clean bores, use this two-step technique. Choose a bit slightly larger than the bolt diameter. Drill through one side until the tip just breaks through. Then finish drilling the hole from the other side.

PREDRILL FASTENERS

Whenever you drive a nail or screw less than 2 inches from the edge of a board, drill a pilot hole to protect against splitting the board. Use a drill bit slightly smaller than the diameter of the fastener.

MARK THE BIT FOR DEPTH.

When you want to drill a couple of holes to a specific depth, put tape around the bit at the depth of the hole. Back the bit out as soon as the tape touches the wood. For consistent depth over a large number of holes, use depth stops. These collars are matched to the size of the bit and a locknut keeps them in place.

⚠ CAUTION

AVOID DAMAGING YOUR DRILL BITS AND DRILL

Drilling is a simple procedure, but it's easy to dull or break a drill bit. Be careful not to overheat the bit; an overheated bit will become dull quickly. If you see smoke, stop drilling immediately. Pause once in a while and tap the bit with your finger to see if it's hot.

Hold the drill firmly upright as you work. If you tip the tool while drilling, the bit may break.

A tablesaw is the centerpiece of many workshops, and it can make many aspects of deck construction go more quickly and produce more accurate cuts.

You can build a deck without a tablesaw, but if you need to rip long boards, cut notches or dadoes, or miter clean corners in your top rail, a tablesaw is the only way to go.

A tablesaw rugged enough for deck work will more than return its cost in saved time and convenience. And the saw will prove its worth on many other home improvement projects.

The accuracy of a tablesaw depends on the table, fence, and miter gauge. Check the table for flatness with a long straightedge. The rip fence on a tablesaw should slide smoothly, lock into position easily, and stay locked. The blade height and tilt adjustments should move easily and stay at the same settings until you move them. Look for a miter gauge that slides smoothly without play in the table slots.

TABLESAW, RADIAL-ARM SAW, OR POWER MITERSAW?

A tablesaw and a power mitersaw make an ideal combination. You can easily make long straight cuts with a tablesaw. A tablesaw also is best for cutting dadoes. With a power mitersaw, you can crosscut long, narrow pieces easily.

A radial-arm saw does what a tablesaw and power mitersaw can, but not quite as well. It crosscuts with less precision than a mitersaw and can bind on miter cuts. Radial-arm saws do not make rip cuts well. They frequently kick the board back. Use your tablesaw for rip cuts.

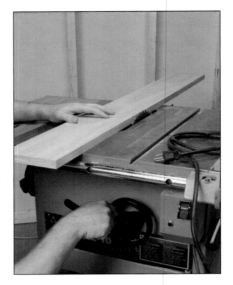

ADJUST THE BLADE HEIGHT.

Before every cut, adjust the blade height to extend about ¼ inch above the top of the board you are cutting. This makes a cleaner cut and helps avoid binding and kickback. If you are cutting a sheet of warped plywood, you may need to raise the blade higher so it cuts through the sheet completely at all points. Always unplug the tablesaw before making blade adjustments.

MAKE A RIP CUT.

Check that the fence is perfectly parallel to the blade by measuring the space between the blade and the fence at the front and the rear of the blade. Set the blade height ¼ inch above the top of the board. Start the motor and allow it to reach full speed. Hold the board flush against the fence and keep it that way as you push it forward. Never allow your fingers to come within 6 inches of the blade; use a push stick when you come to the end of the cut (see opposite page).

CAUTION

SAFETY MEASURES FOR A TABLESAW

Because a tablesaw runs so smoothly and seems so stable, it's easy to let down your guard while working with one. A tablesaw is worthy of respect; it takes only an instant's inattention for an accident to occur.

Always keep your fingers well away from the blade. Never wear gloves, long sleeves, or loose clothing while using a tablesaw. Never reach across the saw blade while it is running. Keep push sticks and anti-kickback featherboards handy and get into the habit of using them (opposite page).

Turn the saw off when you need to free a piece of wood that has become stuck. Lower the blade below the table and unplug the saw when you're done for the day.

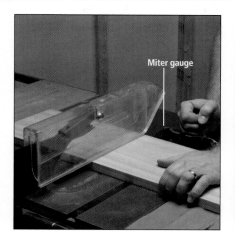

Miter gauge

MAKE A CROSSCUT.

Make sure the miter gauge is exactly perpendicular to the blade; slip it into its channel and square it to the blade (do this with the saw unplugged). Set the blade height to ¼ inch above the board and start the motor. Hold the board firmly against the miter gauge and push the board into the blade. Hold the board only at the miter gauge and never use the fence with the gauge. Holding a board on both sides of the cut may bind the blade and cause kickback.

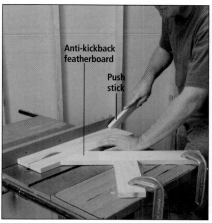

Anti-kickback featherboard

Push stick

USE PUSH STICKS AND A FEATHERBOARD.

To make an anti-kickback featherboard, cut one end of a 16-inch-long 1×6 to 60 degrees, then cut 8-inch-long kerfs ¼ inch apart on the angled end. Clamp as shown above to ensure a straight cut and prevent kickback if the blade binds. Make push sticks out of 1× lumber or ½-inch plywood and use them whenever you need to hold the board within 6 inches of the blade.

MAKE A BEVEL RIP CUT.

To set the bevel, use the saw gauge or mark the bevel angle on the butt end of the board, then tilt the blade until it aligns with the mark. Hold the board against the blade at the correct location, slide the fence against the board, and lock the fence into position. Follow the same procedures for a rip cut (opposite page).

CUT DADOES, RABBETS, AND TENONS.

You can make a variety of wide cuts with a dado blade. With a regular dado blade, sandwich a combination of chippers between the two outside cutter blades to your desired width. On an adjustable dado, set the width by turning the blade hub. To set the cutting depth for either type, mark the depth on the board and hold it next to the blade as you adjust the blade elevation.

If you need to make a cut wider than the dado blade, make repeated passes, moving the board a little less than the width of the blade with each pass.

You will not be able to see the cut as you make it on a tablesaw, so test your settings on a scrap piece to make sure the dado is the correct width and depth before you make the real cut.

Dado (across grain) or groove (with grain)

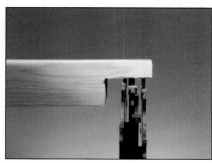

Rabbet

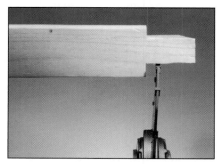

Tenon made with an adjustable dado blade

CUTTING WITH A HANDSAW

Although power tools make accurate cutting simple and easy, sometimes a handsaw is more convenient—even necessary. For example, when you have only a few cuts to make in thin stock, a handsaw might be faster than getting out the circular saw and setting it up. And you can start stair stringer cuts with a circular saw but you'll need a handsaw to complete them.

MAKING CROSSCUTS.

To make a crosscut with a handsaw, set the heel of the blade at a 45-degree angle to the workpieace with the teeth on the waste side of the cut line. Keep the blade from wandering with your thumbnail. Pull the saw straight back several times to start the cut. Don't force the blade; use the weight of the saw to set the pace of the work. Saw with a rocking motion, using a steeper angle at the beginning of the downstroke and a flatter angle at its completion. Again don't force it; let the saw set the pace.

Heel of the blade

FINISH THE CUT CLEANLY.

When you're near the end of the cut, support the waste end of the wood. Grasp it firmly with your free hand, exerting a slight upward pressure to keep it from binding. This also will keep the piece from snapping and splintering on the last stroke.

MAKE A CUTOUT.

To notch the corner of a board, bring the blade of the saw perpendicular to the work as you near the end of each cut so the cutting depth is the same on both sides of the board. It often helps to hold the saw backward, as shown.

USING A POWER MITERSAW

Most miters in deck construction are made from two pieces of wood cut at a 45-degree angle. Miter cuts must be precise. If they are off even 1 degree, the corner will have a noticeable gap.

The most inexpensive (and least accurate) way to make miter cuts is to use a wooden or plastic miter box—a jig that holds a backsaw at the proper angle to the workpiece. These miter boxes become inaccurate as the saw enlarges the guide slots. If you have many miter cuts to make, buy or rent a power mitersaw.

Power mitersaws are easy to set up, accurate, and safe. Some models have a few limitations, however. Standard power mitersaws won't cut compound miters easily; you'll need a compound mitersaw for that. A sliding compound mitersaw will make the cuts in wider stock.

Whenever possible, start with a board that's longer than you need and make your miter cut first. Test it out and recut the miter if necessary. Then cut the other end of the piece to the proper length.

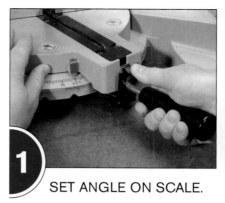

1 SET ANGLE ON SCALE.

To set the angle, unlock the handle by twisting it counterclockwise and move it to the desired setting.

3 UNLOCK SAFETY PIN.

Some manufacturers install a safety pin to keep the head locked down when the saw is not in use. Look at the saw manual to locate a spring-loaded locking button. You will need to release the button to operate the saw.

2 LOCK SETTING FOR CUT.

Once at the desired cut setting, lock the saw in place by turning the handle clockwise.

4 MAKE THE CUT.

Set the work against the fence, start the saw, and lower it to the cut line.

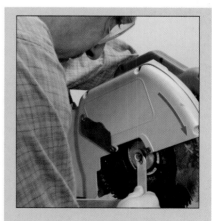

INSTALL A NEW BLADE.

Unplug the saw and lock the blade with the locking mechanism. If your saw doesn't have one, lower the blade into a piece of scrap. Loosen and remove the arbor nut and blade. Mount the new blade, reversing the procedure.

OPERATE SAFELY

Mitersaws can be dangerous if used improperly. Follow these steps to ensure safe operation:

- Read the manufacturer's manual carefully. Make sure you fully understand the instructions before attempting to operate the saw. Ask the salesperson to demonstrate proper use.

- Wear safety glasses or a face shield for protection from flying wood chips. If the work produces a lot of dust, wear a dust mask.

- Power saws are noisy. Wear proper hearing protection while you work.

- Keep guards in place and in proper working order. Don't operate a saw without a guard.

- Wait for the motor to reach full speed before you begin cutting.

- Hold or clamp the workpiece against the table or fence. Never make freehand cuts.

SELECTING LUMBER

Lumber you use to build a deck needs to resist rot, so use one of these types:

Pressure-treated lumber (PT), usually pine or fir, is infused with rot-resistant chemicals. It's the least expensive of your choices, but pick each board carefully so you get stock that is straight and free of loose knots.

Naturally resistant species, such as cedar, redwood, and cypress, resist rot and insects. But only the heartwood (the centermost core of the tree) is resistant. Seal or stain these woods to keep their natural beauty, or let them weather to shades of gray. Exotic species such as ipe, cambara, and meranti are generally more durable, more difficult to work, and more expensive.

Unless your design requires the same wood throughout, use pressure-treated lumber for framing. For posts and framing within 6 inches of the soil, use boards rated for ground contact. Wood that has been kiln-dried after treatment (KDAT) is the highest quality.

Buy the best wood you can afford for decking and railings. Redwood, cedar, cypress, and the exotic species are good choices, but you should seal domestic sapwoods.

Lumber is graded for its appearance, strength, and amount of knots. For structural members, choose a No. 2 grade or lumber graded as standard. For decking and railings, select grades are free of knots, but are expensive. Choose the best your budget will allow.

A lumber grade stamp (page 132) indicates the quality of the stock and its moisture content.

THE REAL SIZE OF LUMBER

Nominal lumber sizes state the dimensions before milling and drying. Actual sizes are smaller. Order lumber by its nominal size. When you measure it you're measuring its actual size.

Nominal	Actual
1×2	¾" × 1½"
1×3	¾" × 2½"
1×4	¾" × 3½"
1×6	¾" × 5½"
1×8	¾" × 7¼"
1×10	¾" × 9¼"
1×12	¾" × 11¼"
2×2	1½" × 1½"
2×4	1½" × 3½"
2×6	1½" × 5½"
2×8	1½" × 7½"
4×4	3½" × 3½"
6×6	5½" × 5½"

MIX AND MATCH

Different parts of the deck have different functions and visibility, so it really isn't necessary to build the whole deck out of the same kind of wood. Unless you live on the West Coast, where redwood may be cheap enough that you can use it for structural members, the best choice for posts, beams, and joists is usually pressure-treated lumber. Build the framing with less-expensive treated lumber, and spend more on better-looking lumber for decking and railings.

SOME COMMON GRADES OF WOOD

Grade	Characteristics
Clear	Has no knots
Select or select structural	High-quality wood. Subdivided into Nos. 1–3 or grades A–D; the higher numbers and letters will have more knots
No. 2 common	Has tight knots, no major blemishes; good for shelving
No. 3 common	Some knots may be loose; often blemished or damaged
Construction or standard	Good strength; used for general framing
Utility	Economy grade used for rough framing

THE BOARD FOOT

A board foot is a unit of measurement for lumber. To calculate the number of board feet in a board, multiply nominal width by nominal thickness in inches. Then multiply by the actual length in feet and divide by 12, or multiply by the length in inches and divide by 144.

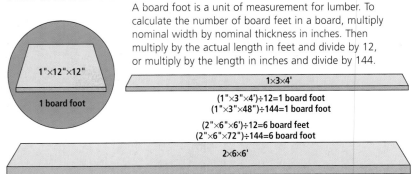

1"×12"×12"
1 board foot

1×3×4'
(1"×3"×4')÷12=1 board foot
(1"×3"×48")÷144=1 board foot

(2"×6"×6')÷12=6 board feet
(2"×6"×72")÷144=6 board foot

2×6×6'

LUMBER SELECTOR

Type	Description	Uses
Pressure-treated lumber	Softwood, tendency to be knotty. Resistant to rot, decay, and insects. Pronounced grain pattern which may raise when wet. Depending on chemical used, freshly treated stock has brown or greenish cast. Can be stained or painted. Weathers to a dull gray.	For framing, interior and exterior trim, shimming, stakes, latticework, and edging.
Cedar	Softwood, can be knotty, and tends to split easily. Light pink to brown heartwood is less resistant to rot, decay and insects than other resistant species, but is more durable. Light colored sapwood is not resistant. Rich, light red natural color. Can be stained or painted. Weathers to an attractive gray.	For framing, decking, railings, paneling, trim, fascias siding, fencing, and outdoor furniture.
Redwood	Premium grade exterior wood, more resistant to rot, decay, and insect damage than cedar, but less than cypress. Vertical, even grain pattern, less susceptible to splitting than cedar. Light cherry red to deep red-brown. Can be stained or painted. Weathers quickly to an attractive gray.	For framing, decking, and railings, paneling, trim, fascias siding, fencing, and outdoor furniture.
Cypress	Softwood, native to swampy regions of the southern United States. More rot-, decay-, and insect-resistant than other softwoods. Lightweight, very strong and durable. Straight grain pattern. Can be stained or painted. Weathers to a light gray.	For framing, decking, railings, paneling, trim, fascias siding, fencing, and outdoor furniture.
Ipe	Hardwood, very dense, extremely rot resistant. Difficult to saw, plane, and drill. Requires carbide-tipped, high quality tools. One of the most durable woods in outdoor applications. Deep brown-red to amber hues within the same board. Tight grain pattern, consistent from board to board. Difficult to finish, especially resistant to penetrating stains. Weathers to a pleasing gray. Predrilling for fasteners is required; stainless steel fasteners recommended.	Expense makes use for framing prohibitive and unnecessary. For decking and railings, paneling, trim, fascias.
Meranti	Extremely resistant to decay and rot. Slightly less expensive than other tropical hardwoods. Interlocked, consistent grain pattern from board to board. Light red to dark red-brown. Can be finished with hardwood stains and exterior oils. Weathers to a rich gray. Predrilling is required. Stainless steel fasteners recommended.	Expense makes use for framing prohibitive and unnecessary. For decking and railings, paneling, trim, fascias.
Synthetics (Composites, Vinyl, Fiberglass)	Materials manufactured from wood byproducts and resins, PVC, and fiberglass. Completely resistant to decay, rot, and insects. Easily cut and drilled, most are fastened with fasteners made for the material. Limited variety of appearances, but some wood-grained patterns are available in composite products.	Lightweight, not strong enough for framing. Most products made for decking, some for railings.

Selecting lumber *(continued)*

How much lumber will you need? For a small deck (10×12 feet, for example), the best way to calculate how much lumber you'll need is to draw a dimensioned plan and count all the pieces of each size—so many 12-foot 2×4s, and so forth. Add 10 percent to framing quantities and 15 percent to decking to allow for waste so you'll get everything you need.

For larger decks, count framing members and estimate decking based on square footage.

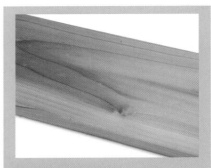

HEARTWOOD OR SAPWOOD?

Boards that have light-colored sapwood will not be as rot resistant as those cut from the heartwood only.

MANAGED FORESTS

Concerned that your lumber may come from irreplaceable forests? Several organizations monitor the forestry industry and promote responsible forest management. For information, visit http://www.sustainable.org/economy/forestry.html

GRADE STAMPS

Grade stamps will vary. A PT stamp will contain different information than a cedar grade stamp. Pay special attention to both the grade and the moisture content.

HANDLING TREATED WOOD

Pressure-treated lumber is saturated with chemical preservatives, embedded in the wood's fibers. The industry says that when properly handled, pressure-treated wood is safe and the chemicals will not leach out of the wood. New chemicals are now in use, but existing stock of wood treated with Chromated Copper Arsenate (CCA) can still be sold. When working with pressure-treated lumber, observe the following precautions:

- Wear gloves (except when using power tools).

- Wear a dust mask and goggles when cutting.

- Wash hands before eating, drinking, or smoking.

- Never burn the wood or scraps.

- Dispose of wood scraps with regular trash.

- Don't use the wood indoors.

- Launder work clothes separately from other clothing, especially baby clothing and diapers.

INSPECT EACH BOARD BEFORE BUYING

If you order lumber by telephone, you will get someone else's choice of boards, not your own. Lumberyards usually have plenty of substandard wood lying around. The only way to be sure you do not get some of it is to pick out the boards yourself. Some lumberyards will not allow you to sort through the stacks because they want to keep wood neatly stacked—the only way to keep lumber from warping. But they should at least let you stand by and approve the selection. If not, make sure that you can return boards you don't want.

Twisted, bowed, and some cupped boards can usually be brought into line when fastening (see page 53). So can boards with crooks. Checks are not a structural problem, but don't buy split boards. Knots should be tight.

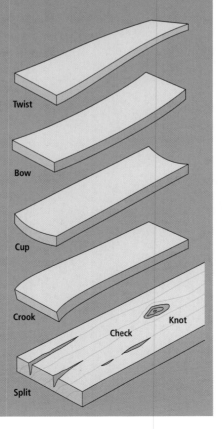

Twist

Bow

Cup

Crook

Check

Knot

Split

CALCULATING SPANS

To ensure that a deck is safe, strong, and durable, local building departments have strict codes regarding the sizes and types of posts, joists, footings, and beams. Many of these requirements relate to what distance each framing member can span without support.

The span limitations of any board will depend on its quality, species, and the spacing of other framing members—and all are interrelated. For example, beam span for a deck with joists spaced 24 inches apart is different than the span allowed when joists are spaced 16 inches apart.

When calculating allowable spans, remember that specifications vary depending on the type of wood you use. Spans may also change for a deck that is higher than 12 feet.

The table at right shows spans typically allowed for pressure-treated Southern yellow pine. The specifications assume that the deck must support a load of 50 pounds per square foot—10 pounds of dead load (the weight of the construction materials) and 40 pounds of live load (the weight of people and objects on the deck) per square foot.

Building codes vary. Contact your local building officials for advice when designing your deck.

WOOD STRENGTH VARIES

Species and grades of wood vary in strength. Design your framing with the strength of the wood in mind. Southern yellow pine and Douglas fir have the same allowable spans and are the most common types of pressure treated lumber. Redwood and Western red cedar require shorter spans.

Diagonal decking span — Joist span — Beam span

DECK LUMBER SPANS

Beam Spans for Pressure-Treated Southern Yellow Pine
Maximum Beam Span Between Posts Based on On-Center Distance Between Beams or Ledger to Beam

Nominal Beam Size	4'	5'	6'	7'	8'	9'	10'	11'	12'
(2) 2×6	7'	6'							
4×6	7'	7'	6'						
(2) 2×8	9'	8'	7'	7'	6'	6'			
4×8	10'	9'	8'	7'	7'	6'	6'	6'	
(2) 2×10	11'	10'	9'	8'	8'	7'	7'	6'	6'
(2) 2×12	13'	12'	10'	10'	9'	8'	8'	7'	7'

Joist Spans for Pressure-Treated Southern Yellow Pine
Maximum Joist Spans Based on Joist Spacing

Nominal Beam Size	12" Joist Spacing	16" Joist Spacing	24" Joist Spacing
2×6	10' 4"	9' 5"	7' 10"
2×8	13' 8"	12' 5"	10' 2"
2×10	17' 5"	15' 5"	12' 7"

Decking Spans

Species	Normal Decking Size	Recommended Span
Redwood, Western red cedar, pressure-treated Southern yellow pine or Douglas fir	5/4×4, 5/4×6 (radius edge, except Southern yellow pine)	16"
	5/4×4, 5/4×6 (radius edge, Southern yellow pine)	24"
	2×4, 2×6	24"

With your plans drawn, you can make a list of the lumber and other materials you'll need to complete your deck.

The list at the right shows most of what you'll need for a 12×20-foot deck, but because lumber is sold in even-numbered lengths, your final order could look different.

Plan your order for the most efficient use of the lumber you buy. For example, decking for the project at right requires two boards to complete each run. You could buy a 14–foot board and an 8–foot board to complete each run, but you'll have less waste if you buy all 14-footers, and cut some of them in half.

A lumber and materials list will make it easier for you to shop around for the best price. But don't shop for price alone—compare delivery fees, and be sure to find out if you will be able to return unused lumber.

PLAN FOR OUTSIDE LUMBER STORAGE

Store wood outside by "stickering" it with 2x2 strips between layers to create air spaces. Use concrete blocks or 4×4s to keep the stack off the ground. Weight the stack to help prevent warping, and cover the stack with a tarp. If your lumber is not kiln-dried, let it dry for several weeks.

LUMBER AND MATERIALS LIST FOR A 12×20-FOOT PLATFORM DECK

Foundation (for 3-foot frost line)	Qty.	Material/Size
Premixed concrete (cubic feet)	4⅔	
Fiber-form tubes	4	8×38"
Gravel or sand for drainage	as needed	
Rebar	8	No. 4 L-shaped pieces
Framing		
Ledger board	1	2×8×10'
	1	2×8×9'9"
Metal flashing	4	as needed
Posts	4	4×4× height shown on plan
Beams	2	2×10×13'
	2	2×10×7'
Plywood spacers (for beams)	11	½×3×8"
Joists	16	2×8×11'9"
End joists	2	2×8×12"
Header joists	1	2×8×6'6"
	1	2×8×13'3"
Decking		
Decking boards	39	2×6×14'
Nails and Fasteners		
Joist hangers	12	2×8
	2	3½×8
Post anchors	4	4×4
Post caps	4	4×4
Bolts or anchors for ledger		as needed
16d common nails or 3-inch decking screws @1,000/lb		about 14 pounds
Optional		
Stairs		as required by plan
Railings		as required by plan
Sealer/stain		see pages 142–147

READY-MADE RAILINGS

Railing style can enhance the appearance of your deck more than anything else. Square-cut post and baluster styles are the most common and will complement almost any architectural style. You can dress them up with mortises, bevel cuts, and post caps.

You can use the stock material at your home center and add decorative chamfers, angles, or dadoes with your tablesaw or mitersaw. But if you want something different and more stylish than rectangular railing stock, look at the supply of milled railing materials at your home center.

There are many styles in different species. Turned balusters are available in many shapes and sizes and go well with Victorian or classic landscape designs. You can use all the same style milled balusters in each infill panel or mix various baluster styles with a consistent post design for more variety. Milled stock is more expensive, of course. You could save some expense by cutting straight balusters for alternate railing panels and inserting turned stock in the panels in between.

Finials and post caps will also add distinct style to your posts. Finials come in a bountiful number of shapes to fit 4×4 or 6×6 posts. Some come complete with lag screws that only require predrilling the posts. Other styles have to be mounted with screws or dowels. To keep rainwater from settling in under the finial and rotting the top of the post, caulk the bottom edge with silicone before tightening the finial.

Post caps cover the top of the posts completely and shed rain from the end grain. You can find them fluted, corniced, and chamfered—in styles that will match any deck design.

DESIGNING WITH POSTS.

Prefabricated posts add flexibility to your deck design. They're made in all material—even vinyls and synthetics. Don't finalize your railing design until you know what's out there. If you can't find what you want on your home-center racks, ask for a catalogue; there may be others you can order.

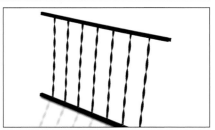

ALTERNATIVES TO WOOD.

Manufacturers of vinyl and wood-resin composites offer some railing components. They look best when the entire railing is made of the same materials. Consider steel or anodized aluminum also. The right metal design can add a style to your railing not otherwise possible.

POST CAPS AND FINIALS.

Some home centers and specialty lumberyards carry turned post finials and a variety of wood, metal, and plastic post caps. Other suppliers advertise in home improvement or landscaping publications, and you'll find many sell their products through the Internet .

DESIGNING WITH BALUSTERS.

Square-cut balusters will go with almost any architectural style. Turned balusters don't. Balusters with a few flutes and collars fit into restrained neoclassical themes. Elaborate turnings look right at home in Victorian settings.

CHOOSING FASTENERS

Whether you use screws or nails to hold your deck together, they (and the anchoring hardware) must withstand years of moisture and the stress of normal use.

When you choose fasteners, you'll have as many choices as you do choosing other materials. Standard galvanized fasteners have a single protective coating, but that coating may flake off and rust. Rust not only weakens the fastener, it stains the wood. Double-dipped galvanized fasteners are better, but you'll get the longest life and best appearance from coated fasteners made for decks.

Nails

Nails are sized by their length, but indirectly. Each length is expressed as a penny size, such as 16-penny or 16d. (The d stands for "denarius," the Roman penny. Some say the size referred to the price of 100 nails of a given size—16 pennies, for larger ones, 6 pennies for smaller ones, for instance.) Choose nails by length; see "The Right Nail For the Job," below.

Common nails, used for general framing, have large heads and thick shanks. They hold well, but may split the wood. Box nails are thinner and reduce splitting.

Ring- and spiral-shanked nails grip the wood fibers and don't easily work their way out. They are very difficult to pull out—good for decking.

Finishing nails are good where you don't want the nail head to show. Use them to fasten fascia and cap rails. After driving them, drive the heads below the surface with a nail set, then fill the holes.

Screws

There are many kinds of screws. Buy #10 decking screws in 2½- to 3½-inch lengths. Decking screws are coated to resist the elements. They're sharp and tapered (for easy driving), and the heads countersink themselves. With a cordless drill, you can drive them about as fast as nails. Decking screws come with a phillips, square, or a

combination head. To drive square or combination heads without slipping, chuck a square-tip screwdriver bit in your drill.

Framing hardware

Building codes now require framing hardware for many connections. These connectors strengthen the joints. Attach joists to beams with joist hangers. At the corners, use angle brackets.

Where a beam sits on a post, a post cap provides a secure connection. On beams, many local codes require seismic ties with joists, which add lateral strength.

A post anchor secures a post to a concrete pier and supports it above grade so the bottom won't sit in a puddle. Get adjustable post anchors so you can line up the post centers.

Heavy-duty screws and bolts

To fasten large framing members together, such as railing posts to

---

THE RIGHT NAIL FOR THE JOB

Use nails three times as long as the thickness of the material you are fastening. For instance, to attach a 1x4 (¾ inch thick), a 6-penny finishing nail (2 inches long) will be a bit short. An 8-penny nail (2½ inches long, a little more than three times the thickness of the 1x4) will do better. But, make sure the nail will not go through the other side of the material you are nailing to.

Equivalent sizes of some nails:

3d=1¼"	10d=3"
4d=1½"	12d=3¼"
6d=2"	16d=3½"
7d=2¼"	20d=4"
8d=2½"	

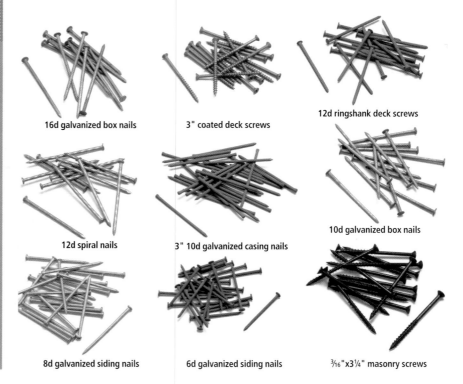

16d galvanized box nails

3" coated deck screws

12d ringshank deck screws

12d spiral nails

3" 10d galvanized casing nails

10d galvanized box nails

8d galvanized siding nails

6d galvanized siding nails

³⁄₁₆"x3¼" masonry screws

joists, use lag screws, machine bolts, or carriage bolts. Bolts are stronger and can be tightened in the future if the lumber shrinks. Always use washers under the head of a lag screw or machine bolt and the nut on a carriage or machine bolt so that the fastener does not sink into the wood.

To attach wood to brick, block, or concrete, use lag screws and lag shields. To tack a ledger temporarily, use masonry screws; they're not as strong but are much easier to drive and don't require an anchor.

LIQUID FASTENERS

Many carpentry jobs call for adhesives, either as the primary or secondary fastener. Purchase several tubes of construction adhesive to help keep miters from separating. Two-part epoxy in syringes is self-mixing. You'll need it to anchor threaded studs in post footings.

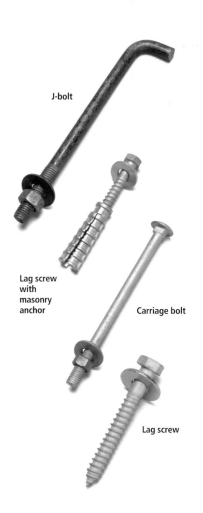

J-bolt

Lag screw with masonry anchor

Carriage bolt

Lag screw

HIDDEN CLIPS AND RAILS.

You can install decking these days without any visible fasteners. Deck clips, recessed fasteners, and metal rails all attach the decking to the joists, either between or under the decking. For information about installing these fasteners, see page 70.

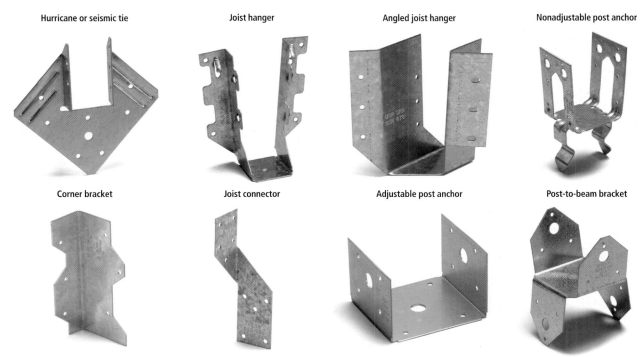

Hurricane or seismic tie

Joist hanger

Angled joist hanger

Nonadjustable post anchor

Corner bracket

Joist connector

Adjustable post anchor

Post-to-beam bracket

Deck footings support the entire load of the structure. Footings usually consist of round holes in the ground that extend below the frost line and are filled with concrete. Different building codes, climates, and soil conditions may call for different footings. Precast piers set in concrete or tamped earth are one example (below). The type and dimensions of your deck footings will ultimately depend on the height of the deck, the types of materials you use, how deep the ground freezes, and the load-bearing capacity of the soil.

Most building codes require that a deck support a dead load (weight of materials) of 10 pounds per square foot and a live load (weight of people and furnishings) of 40 pounds per square foot, or a total of 50 pounds per square foot. All the framing works together—the ledger carries a portion of the weight, which it transfers to the foundation of the house; beams carry the intermediate loads, and footings support the loads that are transferred to the perimeter.

Preventing frost heave
In cold climates, soil freezes and thaws, causing the soil to expand and contract—a movement which can break up the deck if footings are not set properly. Different regions have different depths at which the ground freezes during the winter. It's called the "frost line," and footings have to be dug below it. Local codes will specify the frost line and how far below it you must set your footings.

In warm climates, you may only need a shallow footing—a concrete pad about 6 to 12 inches deep and 1 to 2 feet square. Even in some winter climates, codes will allow you to set posts in a tamped earth footing.

Soils and slopes
Loose soils have less load-bearing capacity and may require more or larger footings than heavy clay or compacted soils. Posts set in sloping terrain will need at least 7 feet of soil extending horizontally beyond the bottom of the footing.

Considering all of these variations, don't be surprised if you find that your codes specify different spacings or construction methods than are noted in standard span tables.

Estimating concrete
Concrete is calculated by its volume in cubic yards. To estimate how much you'll need, use this formula—$3.14 \times$ the square of the radius of the hole $\times$ the depth, divided by 27. Thus, a hole 1 foot in diameter (.5 foot radius) and 3.5 feet deep would need ($3.14 \times .25 \times 3.5/27$) or .10 cubic yard of concrete. That doesn't seem like much, but for 12 footings it would be more than a cubic yard. Two 60-pound bags of premix should fill a 3-foot hole. Order ready-mix truck delivery whenever you need a cubic yard of concrete or more.

USE PRECAST PIERS.

Precast concrete piers are available at your home center and may be used with or without footings, depending on local codes.

They may be used without hardware, as shown here, to simplify construction of ground-level decks. When using a precast pier to support a post, install a post anchor in the center or purchase piers that have the hardware already mounted.

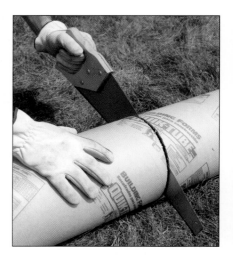

USE FIBER TUBE FORMS.

Fiber tube forms make it easy to cast footings and may be required by code in areas with loose or sandy soils. Sold in 12-foot lengths and various widths, the tubes should be cut as squarely as possible with a handsaw, then suspended above the bottom of the hole (see page 39) to allow concrete to spread out and form a flared base.

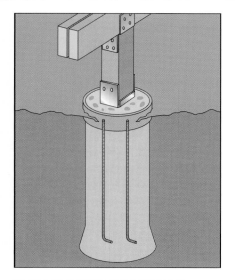

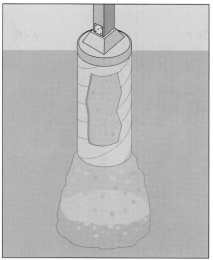

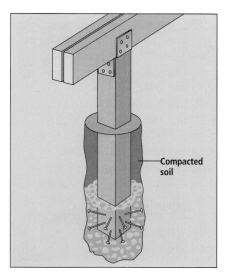

REINFORCE WITH REBAR.

Reinforcing steel bars, or rebar, add strength to concrete structures and in some areas may be required. If rebar is needed, building codes will specify how many and what size. Deck footings typically need one or two lengths of rebar set in the concrete.

EMBED THE POST.

In some areas, pressure-treated posts can be embedded in concrete footings, eliminating the need for metal post bases. This technique can create a stronger foundation than other methods, but aligning the posts is more difficult, and moisture can accumulate between the post and the concrete, leading to rot.

PLACE POST IN CONCRETE FOOTING.

This foundation uses only a small amount of concrete to form a footing entirely below the frostline. The post must be rated for ground contact. Drive nails into each side to hold the post in the concrete. Backfill the remainder of the hole with compacted layers of soil.

MIX YOUR OWN CONCRETE.

You can mix your own concrete for footings. If you have more than six or eight footings to pour, mixing your own can be more cost effective than buying premixed bags.

Shovel the dry ingredients into a wheelbarrow or power mixer—1 part portland cement, 2¼ parts sand, 2½ to 3 parts gravel. Mix the dry ingredients together first, then add water a little at a time and mix it again. Keep adding water until the concrete clings to a shovel turned on edge.

FLASHING.

Flashing comes preformed in Z-shape sections, in rolls, or as a self-stick synthetic membrane. Flashing keeps water from collecting behind the ledger and rotting both it and the house framing. Purchase whatever style that you find convenient.

Finishes,
MAINTENANCE, AND REPAIRS

Once you have built your deck, natural forces can eventually mar its appearance and weaken its structure. The deck will be exposed to the elements, especially the sun and rain. Exposure to the sun causes untreated wood to turn gray. It also dries out the wood, opens the grain, and turns small cracks into major splits. Sun-dried boards can curl and twist. If moisture sits on deck surfaces for long periods, wet rot can start in crevices and joints. Moisture may also cause black, slimy mildew. Preventive maintenance can head off most of these problems. But if they do appear on your deck, make repairs quickly. Put your deck on a regular maintenance schedule and keep this book handy when it's time for repairs.

ROUTINE MAINTENANCE

To keep your deck looking its best and to ensure it will last a long time, stick to a regular cleaning schedule. Sweep the surface once a week to prevent dirt and debris from trapping moisture and causing rot. Scrub the deck with warm water and a mild detergent once a month.

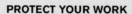

PROTECT YOUR WORK

Sealing or staining your deck can be tedious work, but it will always be worth the effort. Apply sealers or stains with rollers, pump-type hand sprayers, brushes, or pad applicators, depending on the product and the surface. Spray applicators, for example, might work well on large expanses of decking, but small elements such as balusters are better protected by applying the solution with a brush or small pad.

POWER SHOWER

Use a power washer to clean your deck with water only or use it to rinse the deck after scrubbing it with a deck cleaner. Be sure to use a nozzle with a fan spray; a straight stream from a power washer can cut into the wood.

Even a well-built deck can't escape weathering. Unless you want the wood to weather into its natural gray tones, apply a protective coating. Coat the entire deck with a finish soon after you've completed it. Pressure-treated wood must be finished just like any other type of wood. It should be treated with a water repellent and regularly maintained with finishes that help keep the preservatives in the wood. Redwood and cedar also need protection, especially if they're cut from light-colored sapwood.

Consider what finish to use before you build the deck, because the color will be a factor in your design. First consider color in a general way. Then turn your attention to possible shades of that color—dark brown, tan, pale red, or dark green.

Durability and ease of application are also important. Sealers are easiest to apply, followed by stains. Paint takes considerable time and effort.

Consider the wood too. A clear finish is a good choice for redwood and cedar because it allows their natural colors to show through. Treated lumber usually requires staining or painting to achieve the best appearance.

Sealers

Clear or lightly pigmented sealers protect the wood from water damage but don't change its color much. The best sealers contain additives that resist mildew formation, insects, and fungi growth.

Ultraviolet (UV) blockers are a must—they reduce damage caused by the sun's rays. Pigmented sealers offer all of the above protection; the pigment is put in to change the color of the wood slightly. Finally, there are all-purpose sealers, which contain water repellents, preservatives, and UV blockers.

You can apply sealers over or under stains and under primer and paint.

Stains

Unlike sealers, the primary purpose of stains is to change the appearance of the wood. Some stains do so dramatically, others make more subtle changes. Certain formulas offer some protection to the wood, but if you want a full color change and full protection, then seal the wood and stain it (or vice versa, depending on what you use).

The type of stain you use will depend on how much of the original wood tones you want left after its application. Semitransparent stains allow more wood grain to show through but wear away more quickly; they are particularly suitable for highlighting wood grains. Heavy-bodied stains contain more pigments and hide the grain. Some heavy-bodied formulations are almost like paints.

All stains—whether oil- or water-base—including those not designed to penetrate the fibers of the wood tend to retain the wood's natural look far better than paint.

Paints

Paints conceal some defects, can last a long time, and can look great in certain designs. Exterior alkyds are more costly, more difficult to clean up, and slower drying. They can also wear well, which will reduce the need to repaint. Latex paints cost less, clean up easily, and dry quickly, but don't wear well on deck surfaces.

INGREDIENTS IN DECK FINISHES

Ingredient	Description	Uses	Comments
Water repellent	Wax, usually paraffin, suspended in a binder	Prevents water from soaking into the wood	Very easy to apply, but requires annual or biannual applications
Preservatives	Typically includes a mildew retardant, sometimes an insecticide	Prevents fungi, especially mildew, from growing on the wood; repels insects such as termites	Should be used regularly on most decks in most parts of the country
UV stabilizers	Reduces degradation of wood due to ultraviolet radiation	Frequently added to clear finishes	Not usually as effective as pigment in preventing damage
Pigment	One or more ingredients that give color to the finish	Found in paint, solid-color stain, and semitransparent stain	Protects very well against UV and water damage, but ages quickly on decks

WHEN TO APPLY SEALER.

How can you tell if your deck needs sealing? Sometimes the answer is obvious. Old wood that looks dried out needs sealer. But looks can be deceiving; boards that look brand new and freshly stained or sealed may also be in danger of drying out.

Perform a quick test once or twice a year. Sprinkle a little water on the surface. If the water beads up and does not soak in within two minutes, the deck is sealed well enough. If water soaks in within two minutes, it's time to apply sealer.

Just to make sure, try the test in several places on your deck. You may find shaded areas are just fine, but spots that are not protected from the sun may need a selective application.

FILM-FORMING FINISHES.

Film-forming finishes—paints, lacquers, and varnishes—create a solid film on the surface of the wood, but with mixed results. Lacquers aren't made for decks at all. They're not tough enough to stand up to weather and wear. Most varnishes can't take the sun, although modern high-quality water-base polyurethane finishes may hold up on sites where exposure is limited.

New, unpainted surfaces should be primed first. Oil-base primers provide better protection on raw wood than water-base primers. Add stain-blockers to stop bleed-through from redwood and cedar. A good-quality acrylic-latex top coat applied over an alkyd primer makes a durable finish.

Selecting finishes *(continued)*

STAINING PRESSURE-TREATED LUMBER.

Fresh off the rack, pressure-treated lumber has a yellow-green or reddish-brown cast. Left alone on your deck, it weathers to a gray you might find unattractive. That doesn't mean you have to live with this color.

Let the wood dry for a couple of weeks, then apply the bead test (page 143). Apply a coat or two of stain and the deck will look like it's redwood or cedar. You'll have to reapply every year or two to maintain that look.

DON'T WAIT

You might be told that a deck should dry out for months before applying a finish. Don't believe it. The most important coat of finish your deck receives will be the first one.

On a new deck built with pressure-treated lumber, let the deck dry out two to four weeks, depending on weather conditions.

Untreated lumber should be finished as soon as it is dry to the touch. If you wait too long, the surface of the wood may already have begun to degrade.

GETTING THE LOOK YOU WANT

The Wet Look: For a long-lasting glossy finish that makes your deck always look like it's just rained, buy an alkyd resin enamel or varnish that is made for the type of wood and conditions you have. (Some do not work well if the deck will stay wet for long periods.) Follow the manufacturer's instructions.

As Close as Possible to the Wood's Original Look: Apply a transparent stain containing a UV (ultraviolet) inhibitor or blocker. The finish will contain some pigment (there's no other way to block out the effects of the sun), so it will change the color of the wood slightly. If you don't use a stain with UV protection, the sun will change your wood's color more dramatically.

Silvery Gray: If you have high-quality redwood or cedar, composed entirely of dark-color heartwood (instead of cream-color sapwood), you may not need any finish. The wood will turn a soft shiny gray. But the wood may crack and splinter because it's not protected from wet-dry cycles. A clear finish containing water repellent will allow the color to change without cracking. If you let pressure-treated lumber go untreated, it will turn a dirty gray, not silvery.

Removing the Gray: If your deck has already turned gray and you want to change it, wash it with wood bleach. This will not restore the original color of the wood, but it will give you a bleached wood that can be stained to the color of your choice. Commercial deck restorers—usually bleaches—are available.

USE PRODUCTS WITH HIGH-QUALITY INGREDIENTS

Use the chart (page 142) to choose the ingredients you want in your finish, then look for a product that lists them. A better, more expensive finish has solvents, repellents, preservatives, and pigments that soak deep into the wood. They last longer than less expensive products that don't get much below the surface. A paint dealer or deck specialist can tell you which products are the most durable. These will cost more per application—not only more per gallon—because the deck will soak up more. better. However, they will save you time and money in the long run because they need to be applied less often.

OIL-BASE CLEAR SEALER.

Thin and easily applied, oil-base sealers flow readily and soak into the wood quickly. You may need more than one application on new wood.

WATER-BASE CLEAR SEALER.

Latex sealers can be applied quickly and clean-up is easy. The water base makes them low in VOCs (see page 143) and safer to use.

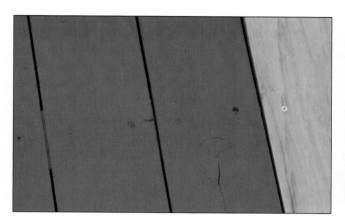

SOLID-BODY STAIN.

Heavy pigments will change the color of the wood completely and hide much of the grain pattern. They tend to create a solid tone across the surface of the deck.

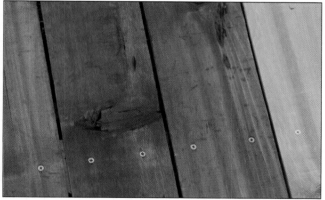

SEMITRANSPARENT STAIN.

These finishes are an effective compromise: They alter the wood tones somewhat, but leave much of the grain pattern exposed.

PAINT.

Apply paint if you want an opaque finish. The best paints bond to the surface but don't soak in. Choose epoxy or oil-base paint for a long life.

SAMPLE IN A CORNER

Before applying any deck finish–stain or paint especially–know how the final color will look. The only way to really be sure is to see the color when the finish is dry.

Test the final color by applying a small amount in an out-of the-way spot on your deck or on a scrap of the same kind of decking. Let the finish dry to make sure it produces the color you want. Paints usually are darker when they dry. Stains dry lighter.

You can apply most deck finishes with brushes, pads, rollers, or sprayers. Pump sprayers (the same type of sprayer used by gardeners) are good for sealers and water repellents. So are rollers; they push the solution into the wood a little, resulting in better penetration. Rollers and sprayers are quick, but wood will absorb more of the finish (especially stains) if it is worked in with a brush. Brushing is especially recommended for the first coat of finish on a new deck.

Apply a finish more efficiently by having someone help you. One sprays or rolls the finish on, while the other works it into the wood with a brush.

Use the right brush for the finish you are applying. Natural bristle brushes are usually recommended for oil-base finishes, and synthetic brushes for water-base finishes.

WHEN TO RECOAT

Recoat water-repellent deck finishes at least once a year. Semitransparent stains should be recoated every two to three years. But these are general rules; decks in different locations that are treated with different finishes may require very different refinishing schedules. You can tell when a semitransparent stain has begun to age by comparing how much color has worn away. Compare the tone of the finish in an exposed spot with one that doesn't see much sun or get much use. A noticeable difference means you should recoat.

Power washer

Paint roller with extension handle

Paintbrush

Garden hose

Paint pad

Sanding pole

Respirator

Safety goggles

Push broom

CAUTION

SAFETY WITH OIL-BASE FINISHES

Believe it or not, solvent-soaked rags piled together in a warm place can burst into flames by themselves. Always dry rags, brushes, and applicators completely before storing them or throwing them away. While applying, wear a mask to protect yourself from fumes.

APPLYING DECK FINISHES

Home centers have a wide variety of deck cleaners, sealers, and finishes. Check with deck owners in your area to see which products work best. Decks exposed to hot sun for long periods may need a coat of sealer every year.

A deck that has turned gray can usually be made to look like new if you clean it and apply a finish.

Manufacturers of paints, stains, and repellents change or adjust ingredients in their finishes, so application instructions might change as well. Always read the label and follow instructions carefully. Many companies have toll-free numbers to call for technical questions. Your local supplier can advise you on which product to use and how to get the best results from the finish.

For best results, clean and lightly sand the deck before applying a finish. Wait for a dry, but slightly overcast day—too much sun will set the finish before it has a chance to soak into the wood.

You may want to hire a professional to finish or refinish your deck. Look through your phone book for companies that restore, finish, and maintain decks. Get estimates and examine some of the decks they have worked on. Compare the cost with the time and expense it will take you to do it yourself.

YOU'LL NEED

TIME: About four hours for an average deck

SKILLS: No special skills, just read and follow instructions

TOOLS: Brush, goggles; optional application tools include sprayer, roller, or pad

1 ROUGH UP THE AREA.

Before applying finish on a new deck, go over the wood with 80- or 100-grit sandpaper to roughen the surface and encourage absorption. Use a sanding pole to speed up the sanding and prevent a backache.

2 CLEAN OFF THE DUST AND DIRT.

A clean deck will absorb finish better than a dirty one. Sweep thoroughly, rinse with a hose, and let the deck dry. If your deck is already showing signs of age, scrub it with a chlorine bleach solution or deck cleaner.

3 APPLY THE FINISH.

To prevent lap marks, maintain a wet edge—don't let the finish dry in an area before you overlap it with wet finish. This is particularly important with pigmented finishes. If you use a roller or sprayer, have someone right behind you with a brush to work the finish into the wood before it dries.

4 RECOAT IF REQUIRED.

Read and follow the instructions on the label. Some clear deck finishes require a second coat. Always apply an extra coat or two to any exposed end grain. Semitransparent stains often require only a single coat; additional coats may cause excessive color or leave visible brush marks.

Good construction techniques, high-quality materials, and regular maintenance will add many years to the life of a deck. Yet, even the most well-constructed deck has inherent weak spots:

- between the house and ledger
- where posts are connected
- boards with exposed end grain
- railing joints
- any notched joints
- joints in the decking

By finding and repairing problems early, you can avoid expensive repairs later. Inspect your deck thoroughly at least once a year. If possible, inspect beneath the deck surface. If your deck is too close to the ground for you to crawl under it, remove some decking boards to get a good look.

Look for soft spots, indicating rot. Poke the wood with a screwdriver. If part of your deck seems to be in worse shape than others, try to find the source of the problem before attempting a repair. Perhaps water damage is occurring due to faulty gutters or the accumulation of leaves or dirt.

If you find potentially serious problems at the ledger, posts, beams, or joists, consult a professional. You can make most repairs yourself, but some are complicated projects.

CHECK THE LEDGER.

The connection between the deck and the house is particularly critical. Check that flashing is in good condition. Use a probe to inspect for water damage on the ledger. Check for fungi, blue or black stains, and little piles of sawdust indicating the presence of termites or carpenter ants. Tighten all fasteners.

CHECK THE POSTS.

Check posts most carefully at the ground line and at the top. Use a probe to inspect for rot by sticking it into various parts of the post and comparing the ease of penetration. Try to find out if there are soft spots inside the post, where rot often begins. Inspect and secure the post's connection with the foundation.

CHECK BENEATH THE DECK.

Inspect beneath your deck. Put on old clothes, and bring a flashlight and a screwdriver with you. Poke the undersides of decking boards, all around the ledger, posts, stringers, and treads, and in any other joints and crevices.

LOOK FOR THE LOOSE ONES.

Loose decking may not indicate a structural problem and may only require retightening the fasteners. Tighten the ones you can and mark the ones that need replacement. If the decking is damaged, remove it (page 153) and install new boards.

YOU'LL NEED

TIME: An annual inspection should take one or two hours

SKILLS: Diagnosing rotting wood and analyzing potential structural failures

TOOLS: Sledgehammer, hammer, carpenter's level, circular saw, line or water level.

CHECK THE RAILINGS.

Railings, and especially stair rails, often have to withstand extra strain. Inspect posts for damage and make sure all fasteners are secure and tight. Look at the ends of all rails for water damage. Replace damaged balusters.

CHECK THE DECKING.

Decking boards split at the ends will often continue to separate along their length. You can try cutting the boards flush with the joists and sealing the cut ends, but in most cases it's better to replace split boards with new ones. For internal cracks, sand the surface and apply several coats of sealer.

CLUTTER WILL ROT.

Dirt, leaves, or other natural debris that collects between the decking or in other crevices can hold moisture for weeks. That can easily cause rot but is easily prevented with regular cleaning. Pressure-washing is an effective way to clean out crevices.

CLEANING YOUR DECK

Because you see your deck change slowly, you might not notice when it's time to clean or refinish it. Make a calendar to help you stay ahead of the dirt and grime.

Little things can have big results. Sweeping and removing debris, for example, helps reduce trapped moisture and the chances of rot. Cleaning gives a drab deck a fresh new look. You'll be surprised how much bigger a clean deck looks.

- Sweep the surface once a week—more often if the weather requires it.
- Scrub the deck with warm water and a mild detergent monthly.
- If simple washing does not get it clean enough, or if you want to lighten the color of the deck , buy a deck cleaning product.

- If the wood is dirty and weathered, clean it with a solution of oxalic acid and water. Scrub an area with a stiff natural-bristle brush, rinse, allow it to dry, and repeat if necessary. Wear protective clothing—oxalic acid is extremely caustic.
- To clear away all the dirt at once—along with any debris, dirt stuck in joints, or loose paint—rent a power washer (with 1200 psi pressure). Clean the deck with a fan-tip nozzle so you won't damage the surface. Used improperly, a high-pressure power washer can splinter and gouge the surface of lumber.

FOR PESTS, GET A PRO

Termites and other wood-borers can feast on your deck. Pressure-treated lumber rated for ground contact should resist insect infestation, but redwood and cedar aren't guaranteed to be pest free.

Termites and wood-borers like to eat in the dark, so they tunnel along the grain lines inside the wood where you can't see them. So, by the time you notice the damage, it's too late. If you see tunnels running inside a board or small piles of fine sawdust at the edge of a board, call a professional exterminator.

Maintaining and troubleshooting decks *(continued)*

REMOVING MILDEW.

If your wood is cedar, a spot of black slime may not be mildew—it could be a natural substance that sometimes leaches out. Just wash it off with a mild soap-and-water solution. If you have other types of wood, or if the black slime persists and seems related to moisture, then it may be mildew. It won't affect the strength of your wood, but you should get rid of it.

Use a commercial deck cleaner or mix 1 part chlorine bleach to 3 parts water. Use a stiff brush to work the solution into the wood. Rinse thoroughly with clean water, and let the deck dry. This solution can also restore some of the natural color to the deck. When you apply the next coat of finish to the deck, be sure it contains a mildew retardant.

REPLACE POPPED NAILS.

As decking shrinks, nail heads may need to be hammered in farther. Over time, however, nails may start loosening in their holes. In this case, carefully remove the nails with a flat pry bar. Put a piece of scrap wood under the bar to keep from denting the surface of your deck. Replace the nails with 3-inch decking screws. Or drive new nails into the old holes in the decking, but at a different angle.

AVOID CORROSION WITH STAINLESS STEEL

Steel fasteners used on decks are usually galvanized to prevent corrosion that could stain the surrounding wood. Over time, most galvanized fasteners begin to corrode. Double-coated and anodized decking screws resist corrosion better than electroplated galvanized screws, but even they may lose their coatings over time.

If you live in an area with particularly high humidity or where the deck may be exposed to saltwater, corrosion will begin sooner. In these cases, stainless steel fasteners may be a bargain in the long run, because they won't corrode. They look great too.

CHECK THE RAIL CAP.

Rail caps, especially cantilevered caps, can separate at the seams. Usually, you can't rejoin the existing pieces. Start with wood of the same species as the rest of your railing and replace one or both sides of the rail (page 152).

INSPECT STRINGER CUTS.

If you have a deck with stairs, pay attention to the stringers. Look underneath or pull off the treads and make sure the runs and rises are not overcut. If they are, they'll collect water and may eventually break. Replace stringers that have overcuts.

CHECK THE PERIMETER.

Moisture can get into the joint if a decking board is not flush with the framing and doesn't overhang it. If your deck has this fault, replace the last three or four boards, spacing them so the last board overhangs the framing.

CHECK THE TREADS.

Overcuts (above), are not the only problem to look for when checking your stairs. Misaligned treads and treads less than 10 inches inches deep can also pose problems. Replace them with new material.

REPAIRING A DECK

It's not unusual to find several damaged decking boards on a deck that's otherwise in good condition. Replacing a board or two is not difficult, and the replacements are more likely to stay attached if you refasten them with 3½- to 4- inch deck screws.

New boards, if they are of the same species as the old ones, will blend in with the color of the old boards after a year or two. But you don't have to wait that long to make all the boards look the same. If you clean and refinish the entire deck, the new and old wood will look almost alike.

Decking boards should have gaps about ⅛ inch wide between them so water can seep through the deck and dry it out after a rainfall. If a gap is filled with debris, clean it out with a stiff broom. If that doesn't work, use a putty knife. Widen gaps that have closed with a circular saw (but don't cut the joists).

If you find several framing members that are substantially rotten, consider tearing down the deck (page 154) and starting over. However, if the boards are not severely damaged, or if you are certain that only a few are rotten, repairs may solve those problems. Consult a professional deck builder if you are not sure.

If a deck feels spongy when you jump on it, it may be underbuilt, with joists or beams that are too small for their spans (page 133). If you have room to work underneath, you may be able to shore up a weak deck by installing a new beam with posts and footings. However, this is slow, tedious work. To add some extra strength, install a row of blocking at the middle of the joists (page 50) and support it with a post or two.

Repair the cap rail

Use the old miter as a template for the new one

1 MARK THE NEW RAIL.

If the cap rail is mostly in good condition, clean the joints with a putty knife and seal them. If a joint is rotted, remove the cap and use it to mark the angle for cutting new wood (of the same species).

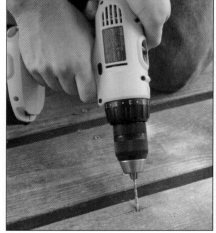

Scrap holds new and old sections together

2 FASTEN THE CORNERS.

Miter the replacement rail first, then cut the other end to length. Snug both faces of the corner by clamping them with a scrap 2×4. Drill pilot holes and drive one 3-inch screw into each edge and two into each post.

Repair warped decking

ADD A FASTENER.

An additional fastener will often bring a warped board into its proper place. Predrill the decking (but not the joist) and drive a screw next to the existing fasteners. Or remove the old fasteners and drive a new set of 3½-inch screws.

ANGLE A SCREW.

An angled fastener has more holding power than one driven perpendicular to the decking. Clamp a warped board down and predrill it at an angle. Drive the screw. You may have to wait a week for the board to partially flatten, then drive in a longer screw to pull it down more.

Remove decking

1 PRY OUT THE POP-UPS.

Pry out popped nails with a pry bar, inserting a wide putty knife under the heel of the bar to protect the decking if necessary (see Step 3).

2 DIG OUT THE NAILS.

A cat's paw will lift most stubborn nails but not without digging up the wood. If the board is going in the scrap pile anyway, pry up the nail about ¼ inch with a cat's paw. Finish the job with a framing hammer.

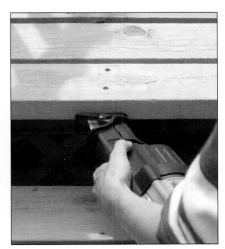

3 REMOVE THE DECKING.

Removing decking calls for caution; you don't want to dent neighboring boards. If possible, start prying where the board overhangs the joist. If not, use a pry bar and a wide putty knife to lift the damaged board out.

Remove stubborn screws

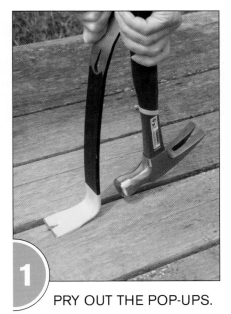

INCREASE YOUR TORQUE.

Working away at a stubborn screw with your cordless screwdriver tip will strip out the head, and you won't have enough left for the bit to grip. Instead clamp a locking pliers near the tip of a screwdriver shaft. Put all your weight on the screwdriver and use the pliers to turn it.

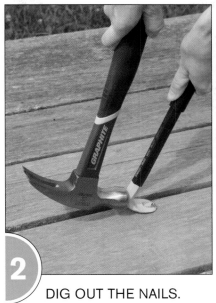

DEEPEN THE RECESS.

If a locking pliers won't get the screw out, drill a ⅛-inch hole into the center of a phillips head. Tap the screwdriver in the recess to create a new binding surface. Then reclamp a locking pliers and try again.

CUT THE SCREW.

If you can get under the board where it overhangs the framing, for example, or by removing adjacent boards, cut the screw with a reciprocating saw equipped with a metal-cutting blade.

REMOVING AN OLD DECK

There are a number of reasons you might need to tear down an old deck and build a new one. Perhaps the style or size of the old structure was simply not appropriate to your lifestyle or landscape design. Perhaps you are planning a major addition to your house—an extra bedroom, new family room, or bigger kitchen—and the old deck is in the way. Perhaps the construction of the old deck was too shoddy, or previous owners did not maintain it and it's now almost falling down on its own.

Removing an old deck is not a difficult chore. Decks are easier to tear down than to build. Before you get out the reciprocating saw and order the roll-off trash bin, however, make sure that removing the deck is your only option.

If it's more outdoor space you want, you can build onto a sound existing deck in a number of ways. If you need more shade, you can add an arbor, an awning, or a pergola. If you simply don't like the way the old deck looks, maybe a new railing or even new decking will save you the trouble of tearing it all down and rebuilding.

All of these options, of course, assume a deck whose structural integrity is sound. If the deck is simply too poorly built or too deteriorated to justify keeping it, then tear it down.

Like construction, demolition follows a logical, safe sequence. Take the deck down in steps, as illustrated on these pages. They're safe and follow a logical progression. Work carefully so you don't get hurt.

If you're going to replace an old structure with a new one, think about how much of the existing material you want to salvage and recycle. You may be able to reuse structural lumber, as well as other parts of the deck. But recycling is not without its consequences. You can pry up nailed lumber with a pry bar, but you're likely to split the wood beyond usefulness. Screwed-down boards can't be pried without ruining them, and removing the thousand or so screws in a deck will take a long time. Nailed framing connectors can be pried up, but the connectors will probably bend. Removing screws from framing connectors will leave the connectors intact, but may not be cost-efficient.

After considering all of that, you'll probably think it makes more sense to dismantle the deck with a reciprocating saw as shown here. Joists and decking that have been cut can still be used in the new deck if they're in good condition and long enough. You can recycle boards for blocking, bracing, and planters and seating.

Order a waste container and set it as close as possible to the site without ruining the lawn. Cut the pieces into lengths you—and a helper—can comfortably carry. Find out what your dumping fees will be—some municipalities charge more for pressure-treated lumber, because they can't dispose of it by burning it.

If your old deck has a water feature or lighting of any kind, find the water supply and power lines. Turn the power and water off before you start. Wear gloves, safety glasses, and a dust mask. Old wood can release mold spores that can get into your lungs.

YOU'LL NEED

TIME: Six to eight hours to tear down a 12x16-foot deck

SKILLS: Rough cutting, lifting, prying.

TOOLS: Reciprocating saw, pry bar, hammer, circular saw.

1 CUT THE RAILINGS.

Cut railings into sections. Using a reciprocating saw, cut the top and bottom rails at the posts. Have someone hold the railing while you cut. Cut balusters across the decking if they are attached to the joists.

2 CUT THE DECKING.

Snap chalk lines to indicate one side of each joist, and with your circular saw set to the depth of the decking, cut the decking into sections. Remove stair treads by unscrewing or prying the fasteners.

3 REMOVE STAIR STRINGERS.

Holding your reciprocating saw so it will clear the joists, cut the tops of the stringers from the joists. Pry the stringer off the landing pad or the toe-kick.

4 CUT THE JOISTS.

Cut the joists with a reciprocating saw, sawing where the blade won't hit the joist hangers. Don't force the cut; let the weight of the saw set the pace.

5 CUT THE POSTS.

Using a blade long enough to cut in one pass, cut the posts under the beam. Have someone help support the beam so it won't fall away when you complete the cut. Cut the posts off at the bottom, just above the anchor. Remove the anchor and saw the bolt off with a hack saw.

6 REMOVE THE LEDGER.

Unscrew the fasteners that hold the ledger in place and pry the ledger off with a pry bar if necessary (it may come away of its own weight). Have someone help you hold it as it comes off so it won't fall and hurt you. Remove the flashing and caulk the fastener holes.

GLOSSARY

Actual dimension. The actual size of dimensioned lumber after milling and drying. See *nominal dimension.*

Anchor. Metal device set in concrete for attaching posts to footings or piers.

Backfill. To replace earth excavated during construction. A material other than the original earth may be used.

Baluster. A vertical railing member, usually spaced between posts.

Beam. A horizontal framing member that usually rests on posts and supports the joists.

Bevel cut. An angle cut through the thickness of a piece of wood.

Blocking. Short pieces of lumber between joists to keep the joists from twisting and strengthen the framing.

Board foot. One board foot is 1 square foot that is 1 inch thick; a piece that measures 1×12×12 inches.

Board. A piece of lumber that is less than 2 inches thick.

Bracing. Diagonal crosspieces nailed and bolted between tall posts, usually those more than 5 feet tall.

Broom finish. A slip-resistant texture made by brushing a stiff broom across fresh concrete.

Butt joint. The joint formed when two pieces of material that meet end-to-end, end-to-face, or end-to-edge.

Cantilever. A member with a free end that extends beyond its support.

Chamfer. A partial bevel cut made along the end or edge of a board.

Check. A crack on the surface of a board. A check that runs more than halfway through the thickness of a board weakens the board.

Cleat. A short length of lumber attached to strengthen another member or to provide a nailing surface for another.

Clinch. To bend the exposed tip of a nail into the surrounding wood for added pull-out resistance.

Concrete. A mixture of water, sand, gravel, and portland cement.

Counterbore. A hole drilled so a screw head is below the surface of the surrounding wood. The hole is filled with putty or a plug.

Countersink. To drive the head of a nail or screw flush with or slightly below the surface of the wood.

Crook. A bend along the length of a board, visible by sighting along one edge. With decking, a slight crook—no more than ¾ inch in an 8-foot board—can be corrected when the board is fastened in place.

Crosscut. To saw a piece of lumber perpendicular to its length or its grain to reduce its length.

Crown. A slight edgewise bow in a board. In framing, the crown edge is placed upward so gravity will, in time, force it down.

Cup. A curve along the width of a board. Usually not a problem for framing lumber. Slight cupping in decking boards can be corrected by screwing down each side of the board. Reject any boards with severe cupping.

Decking. The boards that make the walking surface of a deck. Decking is usually 2×6, 2×4, or 5/4×6 lumber.

Dimension lumber. Lumber at least 2 inches wide and 2 inches thick that has been cut to modular dimensions.

Edging. Wood used as trim to cover the edges of boards, especially decking.

Elevation. A drawn view of the deck that shows a vertical face.

End grain. Wood fibers which are exposed at the ends of boards.

Fascia. Horizontal trim that covers framing right under the decking.

Finial. An ornament attached to the top of a post or the peak of an arch.

Flashing. Strips of metal, usually galvanized steel or aluminum, used for weather protection.

Footing. A small foundation, usually made of concrete, that supports a post.

Frost heave. The movement of soil caused when soil moisture freezes. Posts and footings that do not extend below the frost line are subject to frost heave.

Frost line. The maximum depth at which the ground in an area freezes during winter.

Flush. On the same plane, or level with, the surrounding surface.

Grain. The direction and pattern of fibers in a piece of wood.

Header. A framing member across the ends of the joists.

Heartwood. The center and most durable part of a tree.

Hardwood. Lumber that comes from deciduous trees (they lose their leaves).

Joist. Horizontal framing members that support a floor or ceiling.

Joist hanger. A metal connector used to join a joist to a ledger or rim joist.

KDAT (kiln dried after treatment). Lumber that has been dried after being treated with preservative; more expensive than pressure-treated lumber but less likely to warp.

Kerf. The void created as the blade of a saw cuts through a piece of material.

Lag screw. A large screw with heavy threads and a hexagonal head that can be driven with a wrench or socket.

Lap joint. The joint formed when one member overlaps another.

Ledger. A horizontal board that supports framing members.

Level. The condition that exists when a surface is horizontal (parallel to the horizon). A tool to determine level.

Load. Weights and forces that a structure is designed to withstand.

Miter joint. The joint formed when two members meet that have been cut at the same angle (usually 45 degrees).

Molding. Wood that covers exposed edges or serves as decoration.

Nominal dimension. The stated size of a piece of lumber, such as a 2×4 or a 1×12. Actual dimensions are smaller.

On-center (OC). The distance from the center of one regularly spaced member to the center of the next.

Pergola. An open overhead structure designed to provide shade.

Pier. Concrete, usually preformed in a pyramidal shape, used to support a post.

Pilot hole. A hole to prevent splitting the wood when driving a screw or nail.

Plan view. A drawing that shows an overhead view of a deck.

Plumb. The condition that exists when a member is at true vertical, pointing to the earth's center of gravity.

Plywood. A building material made of sheets of wood veneer laminated with their grain at 90-degrees to each other.

Post. A vertical framing piece that supports a beam or a joist.

Pressure-treated (PT) wood. Lumber and sheet materials impregnated with a chemical solution to resist rot.

Rabbet. A step-shaped cut made along the edge of a piece of wood.

Rail. A horizontal framing member that spans between posts to support balusters and sometimes the cap rail.

Rim joist. A joist at the outside edge of a framing layout.

Rise. Total rise is the vertical distance a stairway climbs. Unit rise is the vertical distance between the surfaces of two consecutive treads.

Riser. A board attached to the vertical cut surface of a stair stringer used to cover the gap between treads and to provide additional tread support.

Rip cut. A cut made parallel to the length of a board or its grain to reduce the board's width.

Ready-mix concrete. Wet concrete delivered by truck ready to pour.

Run. Total run is the total horizontal distance a stairway spans from the structure to grade. Unit run is the horizontal depth of a tread cut made in a stringer.

Sapwood. The lighter-colored recent growth of any species of wood.

Sealer. A protective coating (usually clear) applied to wood or metal.

Setback. The minimum distance between a property line and any structure, as specified by local building and zoning rules.

Set a nail. To drive the head of a nail slightly below the surface of the wood.

Shim. A thin strip or wedge of wood or other material used to fill a gap between two adjoining components or to help establish level or plumb.

Site plan. A map of a property that shows major permanent features. such as the house, outbuildings, and trees.

Skirt or skirting. Horizontal pieces of lumber installed around the perimeter of a deck to conceal the area below the decking. Skirting may be made of solid boards, either vertical or horizontal, or of lattice, to allow for air movement.

Sleeper. Horizontal wood member laid directly on the ground, a patio, or a roof to support decking.

Softwood. Lumber derived from evergreen trees (trees that don't lose their leaves).

Span. The distance traveled by a beam, joist, or decking board between supporting structures.

Square. The condition that exists when one surface is at a 90-degree angle to another. Also a tool used to determine square.

Stringer. A sloping board used to support treads and risers on a stairway. Stringers are usually made of 2×12s.

Toenail. To drive a nail at an angle, to hold together two pieces of material.

Tongue-and-groove. A joint made using boards that have a projecting tongue on one edge and a matching groove on the opposite edge.

Wane. The rounded-off corner along the edge of a board, where there once was bark.

Warp. Any of several lumber defects caused by uneven shrinkage of wood cells during drying.

INDEX

Index *(continued)*

METRIC CONVERSIONS

U.S. Units to Metric Equivalents			Metric Units to U.S. Equivalents		
To convert from	Multiply by	To Get	To convert from	Multiply by	To Get
Inches	25.4	Millimeters	Millimeters	0.0394	Inches
Inches	2.54	Centimeters	Centimeters	0.3937	Inches
Feet	30.48	Centimeters	Centimeters	0.0328	Feet
Feet	.03048	Meters	Meters	3.2808	Feet
Yards	.9144	Meters	Meters	1.0936	Yards
Miles	1.6093	Kilometers	Kilometers	0.6214	Miles
Square inches	6.4516	Square centimeters	Square centimeters	0.1550	Square inches
Square feet	0.0929	Square meters	Square meters	10.764	Square feet
Square yards	0.8361	Square meters	Square meters	1.1960	Square yards
Acres	0.4047	Hectares	Hectares	2.4711	Acres
Square miles	2.5899	Square kilometers	Square kilometers	0.3861	Square miles
Cubic inches	16.387	Cubic centimeters	Cubic centimeters	0.0610	Cubic inches
Cubic feet	0.0283	Cubic meters	Cubic meters	35.315	Cubic feet
Cubic feet	28.316	Liters	Liters	0.0353	Cubic feet
Cubic yards	0.7646	Cubic meters	Cubic meters	1.038U	Cubic yards
Cubic yards	764.55	Liters	Liters	0.0013	Cubic yards

To convert from degrees Fahrenheit (F) to degrees Celsius (C), first subtract 32, then multiply by ⅝.

To convert from degrees Celsius to degrees Fahrenheit, multiply by ⅝, then add 32.